BATTLES IN FOCUS

ISANDLWANA

IAN. F. W. BECKETT

BRASSEY'S

First published in 2003 by Brassey's

A member of Chrysalis Books plc

Brassey's
The Chrysalis Building, Bramley Road,
London W10 6SP

North American orders:
Casemate Publishing, 2114 Darby Road,
Havertown, PA 19083, USA

Ian F. W. Beckett has asserted his moral right
to be identified as the author of this work

Library of Congress Cataloging in Publication
Data available

British Library Cataloguing in Publication Data
A catalogue record for this book is available
from the British Library

ISBN 1 85753 323 3

All photographs unless otherwise indicated:
Chrysalis Images and Philip J. Haythornthwaite

Edited and designed by DAG Publications Ltd
Designed by David Gibbons
Edited by Michael Boxall
Cartography by Anthony A. Evans

Cover image: *Saving the Queen's Colour* by
Alphonse de Neuville, courtesy Cranston Fine Arts

Printed in Spain.

CONTENTS

INTRODUCTION

The former American naval officer, Donald Morris, was prompted to write his classic account of the Zulu War, *The Washing of the Spears*, published in 1965, by a remark made by Ernest Hemingway almost ten years earlier that there was no readable account available in the USA. Morris also professed to find the celebrated action at Rorke's Drift on 22/23 January 1879 'a more satisfactory battle than such better-known events [in the USA] as the Alamo or the Little Big Horn'. Fortuitously for Morris, by the time he had completed his book, interest in the United Kingdom had been revived seemingly for all time by the appearance of the film, *Zulu*, starring Stanley Baker and a young Michael Caine. *Zulu*, indeed, almost single-handedly revived general interest in the Victorian army. What increased the dramatic impact of Rorke's Drift, of course, both at the time and since, was its juxtaposition with the disaster that had befallen the Centre (No 3) Column at Isandlwana on Wednesday 22 January 1879. Curiously, a silent Zulu War epic, *The Symbol of Sacrifice*, had been shot in South Africa in 1918: based on a fictional story, it featured both Isandlwana and Rorke's Drift, and cost some £20,000 to make.

Some histories of the war had been written long before Morris' book, and one of them led to something of an historical controversy in the 1930s. The publication in 1936 of W. H. Clements' *The Glamour and Tragedy of the Zulu War*, criticising the conduct of the campaign by the British commander-in-chief in South Africa, Lieutenant-General Lord Chelmsford, provoked the Hon. Gerald French to publish a robust defence, *Lord Chelmsford and the Zulu War*, in 1939. French was well used to the exercise of historical defence since he had done the same for his own father, Field Marshal Lord French, the first commander-in-chief of the British Expeditionary Force in 1914. Ironically, one of Lord French's own particular targets in the 'battle of the memoirs' following the Great War had been Sir Horace Smith-Dorrien. Smith-Dorrien, who commanded the British II Corps in 1914, was perhaps the best-known survivor of Isandlwana, having been attached as a special service officer to No 3 Column.

In some ways, Clements and Gerald French were simply replaying the contemporary controversy over the conduct of the war. The official history, *Narrative of the Field Operations connected with the Zulu War of 1879*, compiled for the War Office Intelligence Branch in 1881 by Major John Sutton Rothwell, had endeavoured to avoid such controversy but it wasn't possible. In 1948, a professional historian, Sir Reginald Coupland, who walked the battlefield with a Zulu veteran, published *Zulu Battle Piece*, re-establishing what might be termed the accepted account of Isandlwana. In this, the British defeat was attributed to the failure to laager the wagons, the collapse of the auxiliaries of the Natal Native Contingent (NNC), and the exhaustion of the ammunition supply on the firing line. Rupert Furneaux's *The Zulu War: Isandlwana and Rorke's Drift* in 1963 merely resurrected the charges against Chelmsford made by Clements almost 30 years earlier. Then came Morris and *Zulu*, and nothing was quite the same again.

But much more detailed work on Isandlwana had already begun. F. W. D. Jackson published a series of articles in the *Journal of the Society for Army Historical Research*, which appeared in the United Kingdom at the same time that Morris's book was published in the USA. Jackson's conclusions were somewhat overshadowed by the more traditional interpretation of the battle in Morris. Morris, however, failed to shake Jackson's revisionist case in the pages of the journal of the Victorian Military Society, *Soldiers of the Queen*. Jackson himself then returned to the fray in that journal's special Zulu War centenary number in 1979, subsequently reprinted with revisions in 1987 as 'There Will Be An Awful Row At Home About This'. In the interval, Frank Emery had published his interesting selection of letters from the rank-and-file, gleaned mostly from the Victorian provincial press, in *The Red Soldier*. Popular accounts by David Clammer and Alan Lloyd, both entitled, *The Zulu War* and both published in 1973, added little to Morris. A cinematic 'pre-quel' to *Zulu* in the form of the somewhat unsatisfactory *Zulu Dawn* with Peter O'Toole and Burt Lancaster also appeared in 1979.

Subsequently, South African historians such as the late George Chadwick, Jeff Guy, Sonia Clark, Philip Gon and, pre-eminently, John Laband and Paul Thompson have done much to illuminate the war, not least the workings of the Zulu polity. Moreover, the editor of that special number of *Soldiers of the Queen*, Ian Knight, has made his own significant contributions to the literature with, among other books, *Zulu: Isandlwana and Rorke's Drift*, first published in 1992 and re-issued as *The Sun Turned Black* in 1995. More recently, Adrian Greaves, Edmund Yorke, Ron Lock and Peter Quantrill have all produced books wholly or partly covering Isandlwana. Contributions have also been made by professional tour guides in South Africa itself, while *Soldiers of the Queen*, and the journals of the Anglo-Zulu War Historical Society and Anglo-Zulu War Research Society continue to engage with the war and Isandlwana in particular. There have also been videos and documentaries. The most recent of these has been linked to archaeological investigation under the direction of Tony Pollard, which has begun to yield significant results.

That Isandlwana has generated such interest is entirely appropriate given the immense shock that the defeat inflicted on the Victorians – the almost necessary opening tragedy without which no great British venture could be complete. There had been no such reverse to British arms since the opening weeks of the Indian Mutiny in 1857. The public had become accustomed to easy victories over indigenous opponents in such campaigns as that in Abyssinia in 1868, Ashanti in 1873–74 and in the opening phase of the Second Afghan War in 1878. A total of 854 Europeans died at Isandlwana, including 706 regulars, the worst single day's loss of British troops between the end of the Napoleonic Wars and the Great War.

In fact, more British officers were killed at Isandlwana – 52 – than at Quatre Bras and Waterloo in 1815 combined. The highest loss of officers for a single regiment at Waterloo had been just eight in the 3/1st Foot, but 21 officers of the two battalions of the 24th Foot died at Isandlwana.

With the addition of those black auxiliaries killed, the precise number of which is unknown but usually reckoned at 471, at least 1,329 were killed from a complement left in the camp at Isandlwana of 1,774, or 74 per cent. As Emery's selection of letters demonstrated, there was a recurrent sense of emotional shock, especially for those who returned to the battlefield with Chelmsford after the camp had fallen. Some 560 men had left under Chelmsford's command on the morning of 22 January to join various advanced parties of colonial volunteers and the Natal Native Contingent, together totalling about another 1,900 men. The same sense of shock was evident when burial parties finally returned to the scene in May 1879.

At home, *Punch*'s famous cartoon, depicting a Zulu writing 'Despise not your Enemy' on a blackboard for John Bull, appeared on 1 March 1879. *Punch* also offered a version of Chelmsford's laboured literary style in its 'Phrase Book for the Use of General Officers': 'On learning that a Regiment is missing: Fellows should take care – they really should.' *Punch* also offered amendments for the

pamphlet Chelmsford had distributed to his command before the campaign on how to fight the Zulus. The proposed new chapter would be entitled 'How to Ensure a Defeat' with such suggestions as 'Knowing that a strongly fortified camp is the key and nucleus of defence against this vigilant and active enemy, the CO should quietly move off with the bulk of his force, leaving the tents untrenched and the wagons unparked …'

As might be expected, too, the battle was enshrined in popular culture with such sentimental music hall ballads as 'The Noble 24th', which, interestingly, emphasised the supposed Welshness of the 24th Foot when only some 14 per cent of the 1/24th had been Welsh. By the end of March 1879 Hamilton's Amphitheatre in Holborn was advertising a painting of Isandlwana 'giving from the most authentic sources a life-like representation of the heroic stand against twenty thousand Zulus by the gallant 24th', a 'quadruple war dance by Zulu warriors' and other related entertainment. An 'Isandula Benefit' concert took place at the Gaiety Theatre in May 1879. The disaster also inspired a variety of indifferent poetry. Charles Fripp's famous painting of Isandlwana, 'The Last Stand of the 24th at Isandula' was exhibited for the first time in 1885. Fripp went to South Africa as war artist for *The Graphic* in March 1879 and almost certainly visited the battlefield since his vivid painting, which seems to depict the last moments of either G Company of the 2/24th or H Company of the 1/24th, appears a particularly accurate rendition of the topography.

The contest of contrasting cultures was apparent from the very beginning of the war. Given the lack of written records for tribal groups such as the Zulu, much of their story remains inaccessible though there is an oral tradition, to which has been added the imprint of succeeding generations of storytellers, and accounts taken down by the British at the time. The latter, however, tended to reflect what their captors wanted to hear. British accounts in the historical record invariably began with an expectation of victory, the shock of defeat alleviated through the development of an acceptable explanation such as the failure of the ammunition supply and the collapse of the NNC, overlaid with a suitably heroic image of British valour in the face of hopeless odds. Any subsequent British victory, though real, might be exaggerated as a satisfactory last battle to demonstrate British superiority. Native success thus tended to be subsumed and Isandlwana continues to be seen more as a British defeat than a Zulu victory.

1

ORIGINS OF THE WAR

The Zulu War can be placed in the context of imperial expansion in South Africa, the original British interest being the strategic importance of the Cape *en route* to India, the Suez Canal only opening in 1869. Cape Colony had been seized from the Dutch in 1806, the Dutch having held it from 1652. Consequently, there was a sizeable population of Afrikaners or Boers – the latter simply meaning farmers – who had become increasingly disillusioned with British rule, not least, the emancipation of slaves in British possessions in 1833. As is well known, the Boers began trekking inland in 1835, establishing themselves first in Natal and, then, when the British annexed it in 1845, to secure the coast from Boer control, trekking on again to the Transvaal (or South African Republic) and the Orange Free State. A disinclination to continue expansion in the 1850s brought British recognition for the two Boer republics in 1852 and 1854 respectively.

What transformed the situation as far as the British were concerned was the discovery of diamonds in 1867 in the loosely defined territory of Griqualand West, to which the Transvaal laid claim. The local Griqua people, however, presumably viewing it as the lesser of two evils, claimed British protection. An independent arbitrator found in favour of the Griqua and the Transvaal was excluded from the diamond fields, only for the British to annexe them in 1871. The economic blow to the Boers was considerable, both republics being impoverished though the Orange Free State received compensation of £90,000 for the annexation of the diamond fields. As the Griqualand saga suggests, however, there was another significant factor to be taken into account in southern Africa, namely the African inhabitants.

Just as Europeans had drifted northwards into the interior since the late seventeenth century, so large-scale movements southwards of Bantu peoples, particularly the Nguni tribes, had also occurred from the sixteenth century onwards. One subdivision of the Nguni, the amaXhosa, had reached the north-eastern Cape, their power then being broken by the Dutch and British in the series of nine Kaffir or Cape Frontier Wars between 1778 and 1878. Kaffir was the Arab word for 'infidel', apparently picked up by the Portuguese as a way of describing black Africans. To the north of the Great Fish River, however, part of another Nguni subdivision, was a small clan known as the Zulu. They were being transformed by their chief, Shaka kaSenzangakhonda, into a formidable military force between about 1817 and his assassination by his half-brothers – Dingane kaSenzangakhonda and Mhlangana kaSenzangakhonda, in 1828. The rise of the Zulu, so named after an early chief and literally meaning 'Heaven', coincided with the so-called *mfecane* or 'the crushing', which saw more large-scale tribal movements over a large part of central, eastern and southern Africa. There are varying interpretations of the reasons for this upheaval. A period of prolonged drought and other environmental factors certainly contributed, as did competition for land amid overpopulation. Shaka's crushing of neighbouring clans played a part in the prolongation of the *mfecane*, as people either fled from, or emulated, his success.

Natal became the focus of attention for both whites and Africans because of its suitability for grazing cattle. Inevitably, therefore, the Zulu had clashed with the Boers. Indeed, Dingane was defeated by the latter at Blood (Ncome) River in December 1838. Subsequently, the Boers allied themselves with Dingane's half-brother, Mpande kaSenzangakhonda, who overthrew Dingane in 1840, Dingane being killed by hostile amaSwazi when he fled into the Swazi territory to the north of Zululand. As a consequence of their victory at Blood River and their support for Mpande, the Boers laid claim to large parts of Shaka's territorial inheritance between the Black Mfolozi and Tugela (Thukela) Rivers. When the British annexed Natal, which included much of this territory, an agreement on its frontiers was secured with the Zulu, fixing the boundaries on the Tugela and Buffalo (Mzinyathi) Rivers. The attraction of Natal's pastures, however, meant a constant flow of the African population into the colony, reaching a total of perhaps 305,000 by 1872 compared to barely 20,000 Europeans. Not only did land become in short supply, but also the wage rates available were too low to tempt Africans into employment, effectively limiting the colony's economic potential. Accordingly, elements within Natal began to visualise a future in which the port of Durban became a gateway for European goods into central Africa and the colony would be able to draw on cheap migrant labour from the north. In this scenario, Zululand stood in the way. Furthermore it continued to dump surplus population on Natal and to pose a military threat. Natal's long-serving Secretary for Native Affairs, Theophilus Shepstone, therefore attempted to intervene in the protracted struggle for succession to the Zulu throne, which had been going on since the 1850s. The Boers also tried to intervene, their desire to secure access to the sea through Zululand equally threatening Natal's potential future prosperity.

In the event, in September 1873, Shepstone staged a coronation of Cetshwayo kaMpande, who succeeded his father, Mpande, as the new King of the Zulu in October 1872. Cetshwayo had defeated and killed Mbuyazi kaMpande, the brother who was his chief rival, some sixteen years before in a particularly bloody encounter at Ndondakusuka. Cetshwayo was invested with a 'crown' run up by the regimental tailor of the 75th Foot. In return for British support for Cetshwayo, Shepstone secured some ambiguous promises of Cetshwayo's future good conduct including a limitation on blood-letting. Shepstone did not succeed in gaining any concessions for missionaries, who had been singularly unsuccessful in winning Zulu converts. Indeed, it was principally rival Norwegian, German and British missionaries who set out to undermine Cetshwayo's reputation, not least after Cetshwayo expelled them from Zululand in April 1878. Cetshwayo himself had effectively solicited Shepstone's presence partly as a means of ensuring that the British would not back any of his remaining rivals for the throne. Previously, Mpande had not officially declared any of his many sons his heir by recognising any of his wives as his 'Great Wife' until Shepstone intervened to have Cetshwayo declared the heir in 1861.

There were varying perspectives on the triangular contest developing between the British, the Boers and the Zulu. To colonists like Shepstone, the discovery of diamonds suggested that the vision of a thriving Natal feeding the exploitation of Africa was now possible. It would require, however, a new infrastructure of modern communications and an unhindered flow of labour that was challenged by backward peoples such as Boers and Zulu. Seen in this context, the war against the Zulu arose from a desire to establish a settled environment for economic integration and progress. Consequently, some historians interpret the Zulu War as having been brought about by colonial commercial interests interested in securing cheap black labour. Certainly, one result of the war was to draw Africans into the white economy, with which existing African social and economic patterns were incompatible, on disadvantageous terms. The strategic and political imperative of British imperialism, however, still existed, necessitating control of the routes around the Cape as well as through Suez. Between 1860 and 1910 Britain's trade with India was worth that with China, South Africa and Australia put together. In most respects, control of the Cape was perfectly sufficient for strategic purposes. The difficulty in maintaining paramountcy in southern Africa in strategic terms, however, was posed not so much by the rivalry of other European powers, as was to motivate much imperial expansion in the 1880s, but by the politically fragmented nature of the region. In balancing one interpretation against the other, however, it should be borne in mind that contemporaries made little distinction between the demands of security and those of economic efficiency, and both contributed to the contemporary sense of what was regarded as the advance of civilisation.

The solution favoured by Disraeli's new Conservative administration, therefore, was a confederation to bring together these disparate elements, the economic benefits effectively making the concept self-financing. In turn, this would enable the British to withdraw their garrison of regulars from South Africa, which would follow Canada, Australia and New Zealand in being responsible for its own internal defence. Success of federation of the white states depended upon resolving what was often termed the 'native question', essentially the existence of independent black states like that of the Zulu. The Zulu, of course, appeared to have a large standing army though, as will be seen later, this was not actually the case. It was supposed that confederation would create a stable political structure and, by closing the frontiers, avoid costly conflicts between the colonies and their local neighbours. In particular, the avoidance of such conflicts would persuade the prosperous Cape Colony to accept confederation. Confederation had worked in Canada in 1867 and also in the West Indies in 1871.

The first step towards confederation was the redrawing of the Natal constitution in 1875 to increase the power of the Crown, and an attempted round

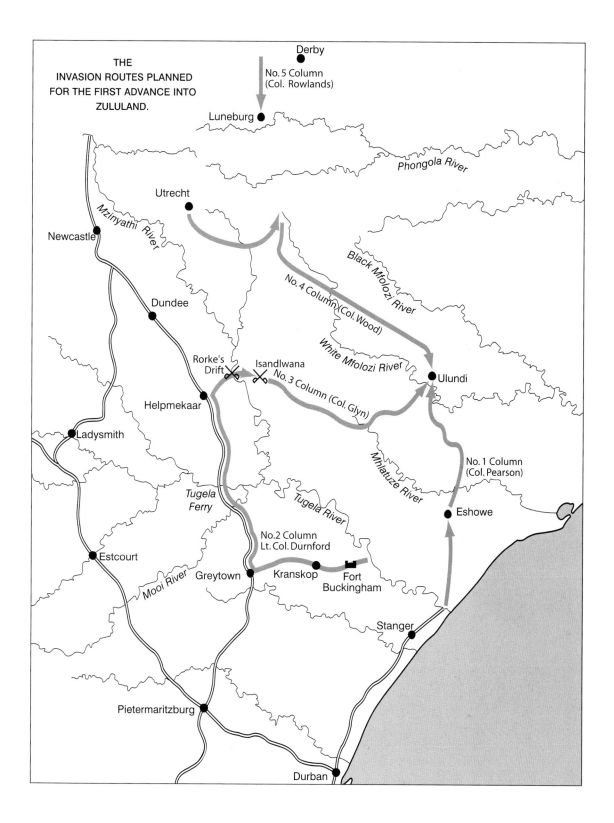

THE
INVASION ROUTES PLANNED
FOR THE FIRST ADVANCE INTO
ZULULAND.

Derby

No. 5 Column
(Col. Rowlands)

Luneburg

Phongola River

Utrecht

Mzinyathi River

Newcastle

Black Mfolozi River

No. 4 Column (Col. Wood)

Dundee

White Mfolozi River

Rorke's
Drift

Isandlwana
No. 3 Column (Col. Glyn)

Ulundi

Helpmekaar

Ladysmith

Mhlatuze River

No. 1 Column
(Col. Pearson)

*Tugela
Ferry*

Tugela River

Eshowe

Estcourt

No.2 Column
Lt. Col. Durnford

Mooi River   Greytown

Kranskop

Fort
Buckingham

Stanger

Pietermaritzburg

Durban

table conference with the Boer republics. The latter failed, but two years later, in April 1877, when a bankrupt Transvaal could no longer prosecute a border war with Sekhukhune of the baPedi, the Colonial Secretary, Lord Carnarvon, approved annexation of the republic. Carnarvon, who had a distinct imperial vision, also installed Shepstone as administrator. The Transvaal leadership somewhat reluctantly accepted annexation largely through Shepstone's manipulation of a supposedly imminent Zulu and Swazi threat. The man who raised the Union flag over the Transvaal was Shepstone's secretary, Henry Rider Haggard, who later would become well-known as a novelist of African adventures. By annexing the Transvaal, however, the British had virtually doomed confederation since they earned the deep enmity of ordinary Boers. It was a reality soon grasped by Carnarvon's new appointee as High Commissioner for South Africa, the 63-year-old Sir Bartle Frere, a former Governor of Bombay, who had arrived at the Cape in March 1877. Initially, the government was not necessarily opposed to removing the threat of the Zulu by war, and elements in the Colonial Office continued to back Frere. Attitudes within the Cabinet, however, changed throughout 1878, with the government facing the prospects of a serious confrontation with Russia over the Balkans and, arising from the perceived Russian threat to India, a war in Afghanistan. These difficulties had arisen at a time of economic depression at home, which necessitated the avoidance of unnecessary expenditure on military adventures that could be postponed.

Like Shepstone, Frere's activities illustrated how determined individuals could hijack government policy at the peripheries of empire. Indeed, the same thing occurred in Afghanistan where the Viceroy, Lord Lytton, effectively engineered the outbreak of war in 1878 against the government's wishes. Frere considered that it was Great Britain's mission to spread Christian government and civilisation, drawing the Africans into wage labour, which would enable them to acquire manufactured goods to their own benefit as well as that of the colonial economy. Thus, he needed little convincing by colonists and missionaries that the Zulu were behind the Xhosa disturbances – specifically among the Ngquika and Gcaleka – that constituted the Ninth and last of the Cape Frontier Wars in 1877-78. Moreover, Frere was quite clear that the annexation of Zululand was eminently desirable. Seen in this context, the Zulu War was very much Frere's war, the only necessity being to find some legitimate legal grounds on which to act against Cetshwayo in what was undoubtedly seen by Frere as a necessary pre-emptive strike to ward off some future Zulu onslaught on Natal.

The legal grounds lay in the promises of good conduct Shepstone had supposedly extracted at Cetshwayo's coronation. The circumstances for exploiting them lay in the annexation of the Transvaal. By assuming its protection, the British inherited an existing frontier dispute between Boer and Zulu. This had arisen over the area between the Buffalo and Blood Rivers around Utrecht, which the Boers claimed had been ceded to them in 1854 and 1861, and an area to the north of the Phongolo River also claimed by the Swazi. Another reason for Cetshwayo's agreeing to Shepstone's coronation ceremony, indeed, had been to obtain British support in this territorial dispute. The link with the Transvaal was also opportune. By resolving the frontier dispute in favour of the Boers, Frere would demonstrate to the latter the benefits of British rule, while simultaneously giving notice to all that nothing could be achieved by opposing British will. Unfortunately for Frere, the Lieutenant-Governor of Natal, Sir Henry Bulwer, was opposed to war, given the vulnerability of Natal's frontiers to Zulu incursion, and in December 1877 he offered to establish an impartial commission to arbitrate the frontier dispute. Cetshwayo seems to have been surprised that the British, who had previously championed the Zulu in the territorial dispute as a means of preventing Boer access to the sea, now appeared favourable to the Boer claims.

In March 1878, three men were appointed to hear the rival claims, namely the Attorney-General of Natal, Michael Gallwey; Shepstone's brother, John, who was now Acting Secretary for Native Affairs; and Brevet Lieutenant-Colonel Anthony Durnford of the Royal Engineers. Interestingly, Theophilus Shepstone's son, Henrique, was one of three Transvaal representatives, who presented the Boer case before the commission, as Secretary for Native Affairs in the Transvaal. Much to Frere's horror, the commission found in favour of the Zulu in June 1878, the usual assumption being that Gallwey and Durnford had prevailed over John Shepstone. The area west of the Blood River was awarded to the Transvaal as a result of long-standing Boer occupation, though they had only grazing rights since the land had never been ceded legally to the Boers. The land east of the Blood River was pronounced unquestionably Zulu.

In line with the new government policy, Carnarvon's successor at the Colonial Office, Sir Michael Hicks Beach, instructed Frere to show a 'spirit of forbearance' and, indeed, expressly ruled out any war in November 1878. With many of his officials still championing Frere, it has been argued that Hicks Beach at least may have changed his mind by the time news arrived in London that war had begun. However, an explicit letter to Frere urging him to desist from war was received in South Africa two days after the ultimatum had expired. In any case, if Hicks Beach had changed his mind, his support for Frere soon eroded after Isandlwana. While it is sometimes suggested that Frere suppressed the report, he actually consulted widely on how to proceed. However, military preparations, which had been begun on a contingency basis, were stepped up despite the refusal of the British government to send out more reinforcements. Frere's eventual preferred solution was to nullify the commission's award by granting the Zulu only nominal sovereignty, guaranteeing Boer property rights, and taking the whole of the disputed territory under direct British control. Since Frere also intended to dispose of Zulu independence, of course, it was fairly immaterial how he chose to interpret the commission's award. The award was finally quashed by Frere after the war began.

It was a number of continuing border incidents that gave Frere the excuse to act when, in July 1878, sons of a chief of the Qungebe clan, Sihayo kaXongo, crossed into Natal to seize two of their father's errant wives and executed them. Other incidents also occurred including a foray into the disputed area in October by Mbilini kaMswati. The eldest son but not the heir of the former Swazi king, Mbilini had settled in western Zululand with Cetshwayo's permission after failing to wrest his father's throne for himself. Frere demanded that Sihayo's sons be surrendered and stepped up military preparations. With the assistance of Theophilus Shepstone, an ultimatum was prepared. Timing was all important for any delay in military operations until the next South African winter (June to August) would mean the grass in Zululand would be too dry and have little graz-

ing value for the vast number of oxen need-ed to sustain any advance. While likely to be wet and uncomfortably hot, the grass would at least be fresh in the coming summer and the Zulu would also be inconvenienced by the need to gather their harvest. The rivers along Natal's frontiers would also be high after the autumn rains and, thus, prevent Zulu incursions. By the time they subsided in March, the war would be over. Accordingly, January 1879 was set for the optimum start date.

On 11 December 1878, Frere summoned Cetshwayo's representatives ostensibly to hear the decision of the border commission under what became known as the 'Ultimatum Tree' on the Natal bank of the Tugela at the Lower Drift. In the morning the award was read out, but the Zulu dele-gates did not appear to grasp the subtleties of Frere's interpretation. After lunch, the ultimatum was presented on the grounds that Cetshwayo had broken his coronation oath. Sihayo's sons and Mbilini must be sur-rendered, substantial reparations made in terms of fines of cattle, missionaries admit-ted to Zululand together with a British Resident and, above all, the Zulu army dis-banded. To add to the insult as far as the Zulu were concerned, the ultimatum was presented by John Shepstone. He was wide-ly distrusted by the Zulu since he had tried to kill a prominent clan chief, 'Matyana' (Matshana kaMondisa of the Sithole) during negotiations over a dispute some years previously. Compliance with the demands concerning Sihayo's sons and the cattle fine was required within 20 days and assent to the remainder within 30 days.

Frere's ultimatum was framed to convey the impression that the British quarrel was only with Cetshwayo and not the Zulu nation. Even Frere's critics such as Bulwer and the Bishop of Natal, John Colenso, accepted the terms as necessary for civilised and good government, though Bulwer came under considerable pressure to put his name to the ultimatum. Indeed, the intention was not formal annexation but the imposition of a system of indirect rule through compliant chiefs under the Resident.

Below: Frere's ultimatum to the Zulu being read to Cetshwayo's assembled representatives under the 'Ultimatum Tree' on the Natal bank of the Tugela, 11 December 1878. (National Army Museum)

Frere took the precaution of delaying dispatch of the ultimatum to London until he knew that it would arrive too late for the government to intervene. The assumption, of course, was that the anticipated swift military victory would remove any chance of subsequent censure. Together with quinine, modern firearms and steam power, the submarine telegraph cables have been characterised as 'tools of empire'. But as yet the nearest telegraph connection was in the Cape Verde islands, and in fact it was the war itself which prompted the extension of the cable from Aden through Zanzibar, Beira and Lourenço Marques to Durban, while Cape Town was not linked directly with London until 1887. Accordingly, it took some 20 days for telegrams to reach London, not far short of the month that it took a letter to travel the same distance. With no reply forthcoming, the British troops invaded Zululand at three points on 11 January 1879. Thus, the war was highly unusual in being a colonial campaign initiated by the British at a time and place of their choosing.

From the Zulu perspective, the ultimatum struck at the very heart of the state system for it demanded the dismantling of the *amabutho*. This was the concept of grouping males according to age in units known as *amabutho* in military homesteads known as *amakhanda*. The system appears to have derived from the Nguni practice of bringing boys together in circumcision groups by age. Between the ages of 14 and 18 youths would lodge at these homesteads and, subdivided further into units known as *amaviyo*, serve for two or three years herding cattle, working the fields and being trained for warfare. In war younger boys would act as *izindibi*, carrying baggage and herding cattle for the army. At the age of 18 they would be brought before the King and formed into a new *ibutho* with instructions to build themselves a new *ikhanda*. Led by appointed commanders known as *izindunas*, the individual *ibutho* served as army, police and labour force until marriage, when their allegiance reverted to their own clans. At that point the man established his own household or *imizi*. In some cases, an *ibutho* might not be composed of boys from different areas, but more specifically linked to a particular locality, as was the case with the abaQulusi in the north-west of Zululand. In other cases, a new *ibutho* might be incorporated into an older one to maintain the latter's strength if the King wished to retain its identity.

Marriage was not usually authorised until the men had reached 35 or 40 years in age, thus maximising service to the King. It should be emphasised, however, that this was effectively a citizen rather than a standing army, whose members spent most of their time in labour rather than military tasks. So unless the *amabutho* were mobilised, most of the *amakhanda* remained empty for the greater part of the year, the Zulu dispersing to their own *umuzi* (homesteads). Moreover, even when assembled at *amakhanda*, their women supplied the warriors with food from their own homesteads. Frere and others, therefore, misunderstood the system in implying that Cetshwayo had a standing army of 40,000 young and 'celibate man-slaying gladiators' whose maintenance was a burden on the Zulu polity and whose continued existence depended upon 'a constant succession of conquests'.

When a unit did marry, it was *en masse* for women were also part of the system, providing most of the agricultural labour force and also being formed into female *amabutho* for marriage. Upon marriage, the warrior shaved his head and had the *isicoco* head-ring of hemp coated with grease sewn into the hair – apparently a substitute for the former circumcision ceremony. The married *amabutho* now carried white cowhide shields in place of the coloured shields they had carried as single men, though some of the conventions were breaking down by Cetshwayo's time with regard to regimental shield colours. Interestingly, the shields were regarded as the property of the state rather than of the individual Zulu. The previously elaborate ceremonial dress had also been simplified by Cetshwayo's time and, on campaign, most ordinary Zulu wore only a loin cloth. Other changes had occurred since Shaka's time, with some men now marrying without the King's authority. The *amabutho* also spent less time at homesteads, only reporting for specific purposes such as the important and elaborate first fruits of harvest festival or *umKhosi*, held each December or January depending upon the waning of the full moon.

The first fruits festival involved various purification ceremonies and rituals to reduce the risks deriving from the mystical dark forces known as *umnyama*. It was intended to reaffirm the unity and continuity of the Zulu nation, but in reality there were divisions within the polity. The Zulu economy rested largely on cattle, theoretically distributed through royal patronage, though in practice the individual's control over cattle was such that the Zulu were not dependent upon the King for the functioning of individual homesteads. Moreover, the ties of the clans remained considerable and individual chiefs within the kingdom had to be granted a measure of autonomy, especially princes of the royal blood (*abantwana*) and hereditary chiefs (*amakhosi*). Indeed, those chiefs with territory along the borders of Zululand such as Sihayo had increased their autonomy through contacts with the whites, trade goods such as firearms enhancing their local authority. Within the polity, too, there were rivalries between *amabutho*. The uThulwana ('Dust Raisers'), a senior regiment with men in their mid-forties, in which Cetshwayo himself had once served, came to blows with the younger iNgobamakhosi ('Humblers of Kings') during the first fruits ceremony in 1878. The younger men had formed some attachments to a female regiment of their own age due to marry the older uThulwana.

In the light of these factors, therefore, the Zulu response to the ultimatum was by no means a foregone conclusion, and the British certainly anticipated being able to exploit internal divisions among them. Although not apparently reflecting Zulu opinion as a whole, several prominent Zulu clan chiefs and *izikhul* (elders) opposed the risk of war and counselled appeasement at any price. They included the chief minister, Mnyamana kaNgqengelele Buthelezi; Cetshwayo's cousin and leading general, Zibhebhu kaMpahitha; and most of Cetshwayo's brothers on the council of state (*ibandla*). Indeed, finding some of his council in favour of handing over Sihayo's sons, Cetshwayo had encouraged the latter to flee to Mbilini for sanctuary. Among the members of the royal house opposed to war was Cetshwayo's full elder brother, Hamu kaNzibe, heir to his uncle rather than Mpande under the Zulu system since his mother had previously been married to Mpande's brother. Significantly associated with the uThulwana and possibly implicated in encouraging its clash with the iNgobamakhosi, Hamu was to defect to the British in March 1879. Another of Cetshwayo's intimates, the so-called white chief, John Dunn, who had settled in Zululand and adopted Zulu ways, crossed into Natal with his followers even before the war began. It was to take the imminent prospect of the dissolution of the kingdom after Zulu military defeats, however, to accelerate the willingness of other chiefs to safeguard their own positions by negotiating with the British.

Cetshwayo also faced the difficulty that he had called up the *amabutho* in September 1878 because of British military preparations, but this had been at a time when crops should have been planted. Moreover, it had been at the end of an exceptionally dry season, which had led to a depletion of pasture and to the death of many cattle. Cetshwayo had little choice but to release the *amabutho* to their homesteads, but the harvest would now inevitably be delayed – perhaps until February. In the meantime, it would be difficult to feed a large number of men kept together for any length of time. It might be added that another potential difficulty for Cetshwayo was that, even if the war were not prolonged, any action would normally be followed by the dispersion of the army for ritual purification ceremonies, sharing of plunder, and recuperation.

None the less, Cetshwayo refused to hand over Sihayo's sons, not only because Sihayo was a close friend as well as a key ally, but also because he understood in the way that many of his council did not that even their sacrifice would not avert invasion. In any case the peace party within the kingdom could not itself contemplate the dismantling of the *amabutho*, while the latter increasingly clamoured to avenge what they saw as the British insult to the kingdom. Cetshwayo tried to deflect the British by begging for more time to consider the ultimatum, but received the response that only unconditional acceptance of all conditions would be entertained. The *amabutho* were thus summoned once more but for an abbreviated version of the first fruits ceremony, administered by the *izinyanga* (war doctors). Thus, they left behind their usual ceremonial finery. The ritual included on this occasion the appeasement of the spirits of Cetshwayo's ancestors (*amadlozi*) by a sacrifice of cattle so that they should approve the decision for war, as well as other specific war doctoring such as the application of emetics to induce the ritual cleansing *hlanza* (vomit).

PLANNING, INVASION AND RESPONSE

Given the difficulties of transport and supply in South Africa, the strategy formulated by Lord Chelmsford was to divide his forces of just over 16,000 fighting men – white and black – into small columns to converge on Cetshwayo's main homestead at Ulundi (oNdini), which Cetshwayo had established on the Mahlabathini plain opposite Mpande's old kraal at Nodwengu. There were some thirteen *amakhanda* in this vicinity. The assumption was that the capture of the administrative and economic focus of Zululand would end the war. By advancing directly to the centre of the King's authority along well-established access routes, it was also hoped to entice the Zulu into attacking the British in the open where superior firepower would more than compensate the relatively small number of troops deployed.

In fact the British had not only underestimated the military potential of Cetshwayo's warriors, but also failed to comprehend that the occupation of Ulundi would at best only diminish Cetshwayo's prestige since there were other royal homesteads. The Zulu state was not like its European counterpart, in which the capital had special significance. The British were correct, however, in assuming that, since the *amabutho* could not be kept together for long, Cetshwayo must throw his army at the advancing columns to bring about a rapid resolution of the conflict. But he apparently hoped to fight a limited war and initially instructed his people not to attack unless attacked first. When the British immediately attacked Sihayo's stronghold on entering Zululand – Sihayo and most of his warriors were at Ulundi – Cetshwayo ordered an offensive, but made it clear that his warriors must not cross into Natal; thus he could continue to present himself as the injured party and avoid any further provocation. Aware from the advice of men like John Dunn in the past that the British had enormous resources at their disposal, Cetshwayo's hope appears to have been that a victory over the invading columns would enable him to pose a threat to Natal and compel the British to negotiate. Overtures to neighbouring tribal groups such as the Swazi to the north, the baSotho and Mpondo to the south, and the Mabhundu-Tsonga to the east were unsuccessful. So was an approach to the baPedi.

As indicated earlier, the baPedi led by Sekhukhune had been contesting Boer expansion for some years, and had continued the struggle against the British after the annexation of the Transvaal. An inconclusive campaign had been begun by the British against Sekhukhune in April 1878. It would appear, however, that the baPedi did not wish to have their aspirations caught up in a wider confrontation between the British and the Zulu. The British were also content for the time being to leave the frustrating struggle against Sekhukhune as unfinished business for the future, Colonel Hugh Rowlands, VC, having withdrawn from the attempt to suppress the baPedi chief in October 1878, in part because of the onset of horse sickness among his force. In the case of the Swazi, Zulu encroachments in the past explained much of their hostility to Cetshwayo's overtures. The fact that the Swazi also rebuffed British approaches, however, enabled Cetshwayo to concentrate on the south, selecting No 3 Column for attack since it was the strongest and the one accompanied by Chelmsford. The defeat of this column would have the greatest impact upon the British. In making his choice, Cetshwayo had the benefit of sufficient information from his spies to know the strength of Chelmsford's army and the distribution and likely intent of the various columns. Spies were routinely employed by the King in the control of his kingdom in peacetime and were deployed in large numbers in the event of war.

The British estimate was that Cetshwayo could call upon almost 42,000 warriors from 33 amabutho, comprising fifteen unmarried and eighteen married regiments, some combined into corps and others forming single-regiment corps. Just over 40 per cent of the warriors were aged between 20 and 30, about 36 per cent aged between 30 and 40, about fourteen per cent between 40 and 50, and the remainder over 50. Some colonists believed this an underestimate, but, in any case, the actual number who mustered at their amakhanda in January 1879 was probably around the 29,000 estimated by J. E. Fannin, the special border agent in Umvoti. Not all members of an amabutho would necessarily be mobilised for the main army since some would often be directed to remain at their amakhanda to co-operate with elements of other amabutho from the same vicinity. Consequently, few regiments would be complete in any one action and it would be quite possible for elements of the same regiment to be engaged in different actions simultaneously at widely separated locations.

The Zulu themselves were often no clearer than the British as to their numbers engaged in any action, but some 20–24,000 warriors appear to have been committed against Chelmsford. A much smaller force was sent to oppose Colonel Charles Pearson's No 1 Column crossing the Tugela at Lower Drift, and only limited reinforcements sent to assist local tribes facing Brevet Colonel Sir Evelyn Wood, VC's No 4 Column to the north-west, Wood crossing the Blood River close to Bemba's Kop from his base at Utrecht. Cetshwayo gambled correctly that the British had no intention of landing from the sea at St Lucia Bay to the east of Ulundi or through Portuguese territory at Delagoa Bay. A small token force of more elderly amabutho was retained at Ulundi itself as an emergency reserve.

Ironically, in view of the British failure to entrench the camp at Isandlwana, Cetshwayo had warned his army not to risk attacking any such entrenched position, but instead to bypass it so as to force the British into the open. The Zulu preference, in the absence of any actual experience of fighting European regular troops, was for a pitched battle utilising the traditional Zulu tactics. These were the impondo zankhomo or bull's horn manoeuvre perfected by Shaka and what has been described as the ingrained Zulu desire for hand-to-hand combat. Essentially, the younger *amabutho* would form the left and right *izimpondo* (horns) of the army, racing ahead of the main body or *isifuba* (chest) to encircle the opposing enemy's flanks and draw them into the chest, itself supported by a reserve or *umuva* (loins). The Zulu did not advance in solid masses, however, but in open skirmishing lines, though these could be 10–12 ranks deep.

Firearms had been available to the Zulu for many years and, indeed, conveyed prestige on their owners. Although the Natal authorities had made repeated efforts to prevent direct sales to Zululand, and the Portuguese at Delagoa Bay were also persuaded to impose a prohibition in 1878, there was a considerable illicit trade. Estimates of the firearms in circulation in Zululand are as high as 20,000, but the majority of these were muzzle-loaders, both percussion weapons and older flintlocks. Probably only about 500 were modern breech-loaders. Moreover, the Zulu were not accustomed to maintaining their firearms in reasonable condition. In any case, few spare parts were available, the quality of powder was decidedly poor, and few Zulu seemed to comprehend how to use their firearms' sights. Consequently, they offered no real military advantage over traditional weapons, which, the Zulu assumed, would give them victory in any fight in the open.

Below: 'Troops crossing the Tugela under the Inspection of Lord Chelmsford': an engraving by 'C.R.' after an eyewitness sketch by Melton Prior.

Each Zulu carried a number of throwing spears or *izijula*, a knobkerrie (club) or *iwisa*, and a short stabbing assegai spear or *ikilwa*, the blade of which was about 18 inches long and 2½ inches wide with a 2½-foot haft. Some Zulu carried the kind of axe (*isizenze*) favoured by the Swazi and baPedi rather than the knobkerrie. Most regiments, particularly younger ones, favoured the smaller hide shield – about 3½ foot by 2 foot – introduced by Cetshwayo and known as the *umbhumbhubzu* rather than the older, larger *isihlangu* – about 5 foot by 2½ foot. Each regiment had its own war cries, but the universal cry in 1879 was '*uSuthu!*', the name of Cetshwayo's faction in the struggle against Mbuyazi. Zulu armies or *impi* were sometimes capable of rapid marches, but carried only a few days' sustenance of mealies (maize) supplemented by a small herd of cattle in the charge of the *izindibi*.

Chelmsford had been refused the reinforcements he had requested in the autumn of 1878, but the government had relented sufficiently in December 1878 to send the 2/4th and 99th Foot to South Africa. Already at his disposal, Chelmsford had the 2/3rd, 1/13th, 80th and 90th Foot and, of course, the 1/24th and 2/24th Foot. The problem for the army was to meet its rapidly expanding commitments of home and imperial defence in the context of a system of voluntary enlistment and a basically anti-militarist society, though, paradoxically, the Victorians were decidedly warlike. There was a lingering fear of a large standing army stretching back to the seventeenth century and the army cost considerably more than the Royal Navy, which had a more obvious value to the Victorian mind. Indeed, the Victorian middle classes regarded the army as largely incidental to progress and empire, even though the army was the agent by which the empire was policed. There was, therefore, an indifference to the army's requirements.

It was still recruited from the lowest elements of society who found in the institution the food, shelter and security denied them in civilian life. Pay was low and drunkenness rife, branding only being abolished in 1871 and flogging not being abolished until 1881. Until 1847 enlistment had been for 21 or 24 years depending upon arm of service and, thereafter, for twelve years until the advent of the Cardwell reforms between 1868 and 1872. Prior to Cardwell, too, the majority of infantry and cavalry officers were also appointed and promoted up to the rank of lieutenant-colonel by purchase. Defenders of the purchase system claimed that men of wealth and position would not challenge the established political order and that it preserved the essential and, indeed, unique *esprit de corps* of the regimental system. In any case, the alternative did not recommend itself to the taxpayer.

Cardwell, however, abolished purchase in November 1871, and endeavoured to complete earlier reforms by simplifying the army's administration and solving the recruitment problem. The solution envisaged in 1872 was one of linked battalions and short service to build up a reserve. Service would now be reduced to six years with the Colours and a further six years with the reserve. Two regular battalions would share a home depot, with one battalion at home supplying drafts for its partner battalion abroad. The institution of virtually permanent depots for regular regiments together with locally recruited militia and rifle volunteers for home defence would also aid recruiting by identifying regiments with a county. On paper, all seemed reasonable, but Cardwell had ignored the strain on linked battalions arising from small wars around the empire, despite

Left: King Cetshwayo kaMpande (1827–1884). (National Army Museum)

the withdrawal of the imperial battalions from Canada, Australia and New Zealand. Almost at once the balance of battalions was upset by the Ashanti War in 1873–74, and by 1879 there were only 59 battalions at home and 82 abroad. The presence of both battalions of the 24th in South Africa illustrated the difficulties presented by Cardwell's system since one should have been overseas and the other at home from which to send reinforcing drafts. Under continuing economies, home battalions were reduced to 'squeezed lemons', with the reserve being utilised to replace young and unfit soldiers in home units in the event of an outbreak of hostilities.

The army's pay remained uncompetitive and there was a close correlation between recruitment and unemployment; one later field marshal, William Nicholson, later rightly speaking of the army's ranks being filled by a 'compulsion of destitution'. The competition of waged labour, and the decline of the rural population badly affected the army: Irish emigration on a large scale had robbed the army of one source of recruits since the 1840s. Foreign duty, insanitary barracks, harsh discipline, lack of recreation, the discouragement of marriage and a complete lack of provision for veterans and reservists did little to make army life attractive to those in receipt of regular wages. Indeed, for many families, the ultimate disgrace was for a son to enlist. Soldiers were discriminated against at public entertainments such as theatres and restaurants. The poor quality of short-service soldiers thus became a scapegoat for many of the defeats suffered by the British including Isandlwana though, as will be seen, short-service soldiers were but a fraction of the British regulars there. Excluding an increase in pay, which was naturally unpopular with the taxpayer, the only alternative was conscription. Conscription, however, was regarded by politicians as tantamount to political suicide and, in any case, was not compatible with the need to furnish foreign drafts for stations such as India. These virtually insoluble problems were exacerbated by the accepted government remedy in times of trade depression of cutting the estimates and reducing either stores or men. As it happened, Cardwell's abolition of purchase equally did little to change the composition of the officer corps, the pre-1870 seniority prevailing and the sections of society from which officers were drawn not altering conspicuously as late as 1914. Low financial emoluments, the high cost of regimental living and regimental tradition did much to ensure the continuing predominance of the landed gentry.

Unfortunately, too, Cardwell's administrative changes did not markedly improve the management of the army for all that it had certainly simplified the chain of command, by rendering the army's commander-in-chief subordinate to the Secretary of State for War. Yet, in reality, a duality continued to exist between commander-in-chief and Secretary of State. The succession of politicians passing through the War Office as ministries changed deferred to some extent to the massive authority of the Queen's cousin, the Duke of Cambridge, who remained Commander-in-Chief from 1856 to 1895. The army never fully understood that their military advice had to be related to party political and economic pressures on government, and was not actually technically responsible for its advice until the late 1880s. Knowing likely Treasury attitudes to its demands, the army always asked for more than it needed to compensate, a process characterised by one official inquiry as a system of 'extravagance controlled by stinginess'.

Despite the tremendous problems with recruitment and administration, the Victorian army generally excelled in its small wars. More often than not, the army not only fought a particular enemy, but terrain, climate and topographical ignorance as well. Transport and supply often had to be improvised and time was frequently limited because of risks from disease or climatic changes. Since politicians found the idea of a continental-style general staff unacceptable for political reasons – a general staff was intended to plan for war and its plans might bind a government's future political options – staff work was also improvised in the field. Moreover, while the practical lessons of colonial campaigning were frequently significant, non-European opponents encouraged the retention of obsolete tactics such as rallying squares and volley firing which would have been suicidal in European conditions. Even primitive opponents could prove to be formidable foes, offsetting the British advantage in firepower, as the Zulu were to show.

The standard British weapon was the Mark II Martini-Henry .45cal single-shot breech-loading rifle. Adopted in 1874, it was so-named for the breech mechanism developed by Frederick von Martini and the rifled barrel developed by Alexander Henry. Approximately 4ft 1½ inches in length, it was a reliable and accurate weapon and was sighted to 1,000 yards. With a muzzle velocity of 375 yards per second, it fired a 'man-stopping' unjacketed heavy solid-metal soft-lead bullet which, by flattening on impact, had a devastating effect on bone. Used with the Martini-Henry was a 21½-inch bayonet popularly known as a 'lunger'.

The standard infantry uniform in 1879 was a red serge tunic, blue trousers and the white foreign service helmet, though the latter was invariably stained brown with tea or some other substance on campaign.

The two battalions involved at Isandlwana, the 1/24th and 2/24th, were not without experience. The 1/24th had been overseas since 1867 and in South Africa since 1875, and had a large proportion of long-service men enlisted prior to the introduction of short service. Officers and NCOs had considerable continuity of service with the battalion and it had performed well against the Xhosa in the Transkei campaign of 1877–78. Two reinforced companies had broken up a force of some 5–6,000 Gcaleka and Ngquika tribesmen with disciplined musketry at Quintana (Kwa Centane) on 7 February 1878. While the 2/24th had a higher proportion of younger short-service soldiers – and more Welshmen than the 1/24th – and had not arrived in South Africa until 1878, it had also been tested against the Gaikas in the Ninth Cape Frontier War. Not unusually, given its long overseas service, the strength of the 1/24th was somewhat below establishment at 700 other ranks; the 2/24th had about 830. It was unusual for two battalions of the same regiment to serve side by side and contacts at least between officers were renewed, and they dined together before entering Zululand on the anniversary of the battle of Chillianwallah in the Second Sikh War (13 January 1849). On that occasion, the 24th had lost their Queen's Colour though the Regimental Colour had been saved. In addition, thirteen officers were killed (the bodies being laid out on the mess table) and nine wounded. Ironically, Captain William Degacher of the 1/24th proposed the toast that 'we may not get into such a mess, and have better luck this time'. William's elder brother, Brevet Lieutenant-Colonel Henry Degacher, commanded the 2/24th.

Chelmsford lacked mounted troops and, as a result, men detached from the infantry battalions – the 2/3rd, 1/13th, 1/24th and 80th – formed two squadrons of Imperial Mounted Infantry, one of these having been first raised for the campaign against Sekhukhune. In addition, Chelmsford drew on colonial volunteer units, eight of the fifteen Natal volunteer units existing in 1879 agreeing to serve beyond the boundary of Natal. He also drew on the Natal Mounted Police. Similarly, other irregular units were raised. Some, like the Frontier Light Horse, had been formed for the campaign against Sekhukhune and were retained, Chelmsford holding out the prospect of land in Zululand after the successful conclusion of the war as an unauthorised inducement. Some 170 men were also sent ashore from HMS *Active* as a naval brigade. In all, Chelmsford had 5,476 regulars and 1,193 irregular horsemen.

It was still considered that the force was insufficient and, at the suggestion of Durnford, the Natal Native Contingent was formed from African levies. The use of African levies was not new, the Cape Mounted Rifles having been recruited among the 'Hottentots' (Khikhoi) between 1827 and 1851 and the Mfengu having been used against the Xhosa in both the Eighth and Ninth Frontier Wars. Chelmsford's successor, Sir Garnet Wolseley, would also use some 10,000 Swazis against Sekhukhune in 1879–80. Initially, however, the raising of the NNC was opposed by Bulwer, who disliked the prospect of war generally and felt that the raising of native levies was an unnecessary provocation to the Zulu. Consequently the NNC was not recruited until November 1878 and only some six weeks elapsed before they were sent on campaign.

Seven battalions were raised through the efforts of Resident Magistrates, organised in three regiments, the 1st NNC having three battalions, the 2nd and 3rd NNC two each. Each battalion was divided into ten companies of approximately 100 men. Because of concern expressed by settlers, only one in ten were armed, the remainder carrying their own traditional weapons, a red headband being all that distinguished them from hostile Zulu. In the case of the 1/3rd NNC, moreover, it seems that only half the rifles handed out were the Martini-Henry, the remainder being old Enfield muzzle-loaders. Seconded regulars or former regulars were appointed as officers and other whites as NCOs, each company having three officers – a captain and two lieutenants – and six NCOs. While the officers were frequently respectable and often spoke local languages – though not necessarily those of their levies – most of the NCOs were from the dregs of Natal society. One NNC battalion commander, Commandant George Hamilton-Browne, himself a colourful and uncompromising figure, characterised his NCOs as 'an awful tough crowd'.

The local chiefs all owed recognition of their official positions to their allegiance to the British, each receiving a government stipend. Many were also hos-

Left: A trooper of one of the irregular colonial mounted units accompanying Chelmsford's column.

tile to the Zulu, peoples like the amaHlubi, amaNgwane, abaThembu and amaQwabe having been driven into Natal by the Zulu in the past. Others, like the amaChunu of Chief Pakhade, had long fought against Zulu domination. Indeed, Pakhade's son, Gabangaye, was to lead the amaChunu contingent in the NNC. The 3rd Regiment of the NNC, which accompanied No 3 Column to Isandlwana, for example, was recruited from the abaThembu, amaChunu, amaBhele, and iziGquoza. The latter were Zulu exiled as a result of Cetshwayo's victory over his half-brother in 1856, their chief being another of Cetshwayo's brothers, Sikhotha kaMpande. Most of the regiment came from Weenen County, but others came from Klip River County near Ladysmith. The 1st Regiment, which accompanied Durnford's No 2 Column, were raised from amaNgwane, amaBaso, amaNyuswa, abaseMbo, amaBomvu, amaChunu and abaThembu. Few if any had military training even in traditional warfare, most having only taken part in mock conflicts at feast times. The men themselves received a free blanket, a daily ration of meat and maize, and a sum of £1.2s.0d a month.

Five troops of Natal Native Horse were also raised, three recruited from the amaNgwane of the Drakensberg foothills, descendants of those driven westwards by the effects of the *mfecane* and traditional enemies of the Zulu. These troops were known to the British as the Sikali Horse after their chief, Zikhali kaMatiwane. The other two troops were the Edendale Troop and the Hlubi Troop. The former were Christian converts from the Edendale Mission, a Wesleyan establishment. They were led by Simeon Kambule, son of a large landowner who had been killed beside Durnford in the campaign against the amaHlubi of Langalibalele kaMthimkhulu in 1873. The latter had defied the Natal authorities by declining to register firearms obtained by some of his tribesmen as wages in kind while working in the diamond fields. The Hlubi Troop were Tlokwa, a sub-division of the baSotho (Basuto) people from Weenen County, who had previously served with Durnford against Langalibalele's amaHlubi, and were led, confusingly, by Hlubi Molife. Only the latter were baSotho but the British also tended to refer to the Sikali Horse as Basuto.

Three companies of Natal Native Pioneers and a variety of black border guards were raised, and border levies for those districts whose boundaries lay on the Buffalo and Tugela Rivers. Raised under Bulwer's authority as Lieutenant-Governor, these border levies were to become the focus of a dispute between him and Chelmsford after Isandlwana when Chelmsford wanted them committed to raiding Zululand. In all, 9,350 black auxiliaries were to accompany the invading columns, and more than 6,000 were enrolled in the border guards and levies.

In assembling this force, it was not the case that the British had no knowledge of the Zulu. As indicated already, Chelmsford had issued a pamphlet on Zulu tactics written by a border agent, Frederick Fynney, in November 1878. It was popularly known as 'Bellairs Mixture', Bellairs being the name of Chelmsford's Deputy Adjutant-General as well as a patent medicine. Fynney's pamphlet, however, was not always a reliable source on the Zulu army, sometimes confusing the names of an *ibutho* with those of an *ikhanda*, as well as tending to give only one name to an *ibutho* when, on occasions, more than one alternative was possible. Chelmsford, however, also took care to issue Field Regulations specifying how to fight the Zulu as well as detailed tactical instructions to his column commanders.

While the precise number of warriors at Cetshwayo's disposal may have been under-estimated, Chelmsford's strategy in using three columns – Nos. 1, 3 and 4 – to enter Zululand was intended to divide the Zulu forces as well as to destroy as many *amakhanda* as possible, thus systematically reducing the Zulu capacity to resist by destroying crops and livestock. In the event, Chelmsford was restricted by the limited access to Zululand from Natal – at the Lower, Middle and Rorke's Drifts. A distance of 105 miles separated the Lower Drift from the Middle Drift, Rorke's Drift lying between them. Two further columns – No 2 Column under Durnford, initially at Kranskop to cover the Middle Drift over the Tugela; and No 5 Column at Luneburg under Rowlands – were to be kept in reserve to prevent any Zulu counter-incursion into Natal. It was also intended that Rowlands keep a wary eye on the Swazi and any dissident Boers. Disgusted with the decision of the boundary commission, few Boers were prepared to assist the British in the coming campaign and most remained distinctly hostile. As it happened, the three invading columns would also provide cover for vulnerable points in Natal and the Transvaal, Pearson covering the coastal plain, Wood the Transvaal and Chelmsford himself central Natal.

Moreover, as already indicated, the timing of the British invasion was well judged. Chelmsford was not quite the outright fool sometimes imagined though he greatly under-estimated the Zulu as an opponent. Now 52, Frederick Augustus Thesiger had seen active service in the Crimea, the Mutiny and Abyssinia, moving to the South African command from being Adjutant-General in India. He succeeded his father as Second Baron Chelmsford in October 1878. Against the Xhosa, Chelmsford had proved equal to the task of fighting guerrilla opponents in difficult terrain, and the Zulu, it was assumed, would fight in the open. Tall and thin, a teetotaller, keen on amateur dramatics and an accomplished clarinettist, he was regarded as competent and reliable, as well as being decent and tactful. He had showed some flair for handling the often-difficult colonial contingents. He was also undoubtedly conscientious and worked hard to gather his forces and make the necessary arrangements for the coming campaign.

Unfortunately, however, Chelmsford was conservative in his military opinions, prone to sudden changes of mind, and over-influenced by his assistant military secretary, Brevet Lieutenant- Colonel John North Crealock. Although a talented artist, the 42- year-old Crealock was well described by Bulwer as 'a sort of military wasp', excelling in his arrogance and snobbishness. Paradoxically, despite his reliance upon Crealock, Chelmsford found it difficult to delegate and, in any case, his personal staff in Zululand was pitifully small, comprising just four officers. Indeed, Chelmsford had no intelligence officer on his staff at all. Eventually, he appointed a civilian with local knowledge, the Hon. William Drummond, but not until May 1879. Drummond, however, accompanied Chelmsford into Zululand as an interpreter. Drummond and other civilians who accompanied the invading columns such as the border magistrate, Henry Francis Fynn, were familiar with the Zulu and Zululand, but there were no adequate maps and so Chelmsford lacked reliable military knowledge of the topography of the interior.

His great problem was lack of transport, which led to the decision to deploy only three of the five columns in Zululand. He had hoped to persuade Bulwer to

Below: 'En Route to the Zulu War': piper and officers of the 91st Highlanders. An engraving by 'C.R.' after an eyewitness sketch by Melton Prior

impose martial law, thereby enabling him to commandeer wagons and oxen, but Bulwer refused so Chelmsford was obliged to purchase or hire the necessary transport. This naturally drove up prices alarmingly, not only for livestock but also for drivers, as did the subsequent decision to pay generous compensation for any wagons and livestock lost in Zululand. The average price of a wagon reached £100 for purchase and £90 per month for hire, and the purchase price for horses averaged £27, mules £23 and oxen £17.

Ultimately, Chelmsford managed to collect 977 wagons, 56 carts, 10,023 oxen, 803 horses and 398 mules. No fewer than sixteen oxen were required to pull each wagon under the supervision of a driver and African *voorloopers*, who assisted the driver in guiding the lead animals. Consequently, some 1,910 assorted civilian conductors, drivers and *voorloopers* accompanied Chelmsford's columns.

One of the four Major-Generals sent out to assist Chelmsford after Isandlwana, the Hon. Henry Hugh Clifford, VC, attributed the soaring cost of the war – the official total was £5.2 million, but Clifford suspected the actual total in excess of £8 million – largely to the general inefficiency of the civilian Commissary-General, Edward Strickland. Contrary to the usual regulations which stipulated that the Commissariat control all transport, Chelmsford had formed a separate transport department and gave each column its own seconded regular as transport officer, but he continued to use Strickland as the conduit for orders sent to his transport directors. Chelmsford also failed to develop an adequate system of depots, so each column was obliged to carry most of its own requirements, in some respects making each column an escort for its own food. Isandlwana, indeed, was to cripple No 3 Column for the loss of the camp meant also the loss of 132 wagons, hundreds of oxen, and £60,000 worth of supplies.

Even given sufficient transport, campaigning would inevitably be slow for oxen could make at best only eleven miles a day and had to be rested every three to four hours and grazed for five or six hours. Back in June 1878 it had taken a small column of just five companies, four guns and some mounted infantry led by Evelyn Wood some five hours to get across the Kei River on a march from King William's Town to Utrecht. In March 1879 during the relief of Pearson at Eshowe, it would take Chelmsford nine hours to cross the Amatukulu River. Carrying up to 8,000 pounds of supplies (though 2–3,000 was more usual on tracks such as those in Zululand), each wagon required at least 40 yards of road, and on bad tracks 60 yards was allowed. Thus, Sir Garnet Wolseley was later to suggest that, during the second invasion of Zululand, Chelmsford's wagon train stretched three or four miles further than the column could march in a day.

Assembling at Helpmekaar on the main wagon track from Pietermaritzburg down to Rorke's Drift, No 3 Column was nominally commanded by the 49-year-old Brevet Colonel Richard Glyn of the 1/24th. Major Francis Clery, former Professor of Tactics at the Royal Military College and future Commandant of the Staff College, was Glyn's chief of staff. Not unlike Crealock, Clery was an acerbic character and, not surprisingly, he and Crealock did not get on. Moreover as

Chelmsford also chose to accompany the column, Glyn and Clery found themselves reduced to ciphers to the extent that Glyn, a man of very short stature, became all but invisible, invariably referring Clery directly to Chelmsford whenever any need for decisions arose. Indeed Clery was to complain later that he and Glyn, who anyway tended to the lethargic, were only permitted to post the guards and 'all interesting work of that kind'. Crealock's post-facto defence of Chelmsford, and that of Chelmsford himself, was to try to maintain that, since Glyn and not Chelmsford had commanded the Column, Glyn must be to blame. In response, Clery told Sir Archibald Alison of the War Office Intelligence Branch that Glyn 'commanded nothing except myself and another functionary called his "orderly officer"'. The latter was Lieutenant Neville Coghill of the 1/24th.

Glyn's Column totalled 4,313 combatants, with 220 wagons, 82 carts, 1,507 oxen, 49 baggage horses, 67 mules and 346 assorted conductors, drivers and *voorloopers*. The regular infantry element consisted of seven companies of the 1/24th under Brevet Lieutenant-Colonel Henry Pulleine; and eight companies of the 2/24th under Henry Degacher. In support, there was N Battery, 5th Brigade, Royal Artillery, with its six 7-pounder RML (rifled muzzle-loading) guns, under Brevet Lieutenant-Colonel Arthur Harness; and elements of No 5 Company, Royal Engineers. Having no regular cavalry, the regular mounted element consisted of 111 men of the 1st Squadron, Imperial Mounted Infantry, drawn from various regiments and commanded by Brevet Major Cecil Russell. There were also two battalions of the 3rd NNC, commanded by Commandant Rupert Lonsdale, the 1/3rd commanded by Hamilton-Browne and the 2/3rd by Commandant A. W. Cooper; and a company of Natal Native Pioneers under Captain J. Nolan. The colonial units comprised the 130 men of the Natal Mounted Police under Inspector George Mansel, and a squadron of mounted colonial volunteers. The latter comprised the 60 men of the Natal Carbineers led by Captain 'Offy' Shepstone, another of the sons of Theophilus Shepstone; the 30-strong Newcastle Mounted Rifles, led by Captain Robert Bradstreet; and the 23-strong Buffalo Border Guard, led by Captain Tom Smith. Both the Newcastle Mounted Rifles and the Buffalo Border Guard came from the Newcastle Division of northern Natal, the former raised in 1875 and the latter two years earlier.

Chelmsford effected one change in the command arrangements before the column entered Zululand, placing Russell in command of all mounted troops rather than Major John Dartnell, a former regular, who had raised the Natal Mounted Police in 1874 and was theoretically designated as Commandant of Volunteers. In the event, the colonial volunteers so resented Russell's elevation over the popular Dartnell that Chelmsford was compelled to promote Dartnell and nominally accord him a place on his own staff so that, in theory, he exercised command over Russell, who also received local rank as Lieutenant-Colonel.

3
THE ADVANCE INTO ZULULAND

The Column crossed the Buffalo River at Rorke's Drift on 11 January, leaving B Company, 2/24th as garrison under Lieutenant Gonville ('Gonny') Bromhead, the post as a whole being under the command of Brevet Major Henry Spalding of the 104th Foot. It has sometimes been suggested that Bromhead's company was chosen for the assignment because of his deafness, but other companies of the regiment also remained on detached service. Moreover, it was intended that B Company would move up to join the Column in due course.

As indicated previously, on 12 January there was brief action against some of Sihayo's followers at his kraal at Kwa Sokhexe overlooking the Batshe valley. On the 17th, Chelmsford decided to make his next camp at Isandlwana, a site initially reconnoitred by Cecil Russell, some ten miles beyond Rorke's Drift. It was the only area in the vicinity that offered sufficient space for the transport and animals, while allowing its defenders a seemingly reasonable field of fire. It also had plentiful brushwood for fires and water supplies close at hand. The recent heavy rains made progress hard going and repairs to the track were required to enable the wagons to reach the new camp, these only being completed in time for the lead elements of the Column to move to Isandlwana on 20 January. Not only had the rains made the going especially difficult, but it had also delayed, in turn, the bringing up of further supplies to Rorke's Drift. Chelmsford wrote to Pearson on 15 January of 'having an impassable morass in our front and an empty supply depot in our rear'. He had been reluctant, therefore, to go more than about eight miles from Rorke's Drift until the road could be improved. On the 20th he made a reconnaissance beyond the new camp, during the course of which Glyn's orderly officer, Coghill, fell from his horse and badly wrenched his knee trying to catch a chicken, the knee having already been injured earlier by an assegai thrust during some horseplay in the officers' mess.

In Zulu Isandlwana means literally 'shaped something like a small hut', but it was actually named for its similarity to the second stomach of a ruminant. As is well known, many of the 24th commented on the similarity between Isandlwana and their own regimental badge, a sphinx, granted for distinguished service in Egypt in 1801. At the time, it might be noted, Isandlwana was variously spelled in British reports, versions including Isandula, Insalwana, Insilwana, Isandlana, Insandwhlana, Insandlwana, Sandoola, Sanhlana, Sandula and Sandhlwana. Until relatively recently, it was commonly rendered as Isandhlwana. To the north of the camp site, established under the shadow of Isandlwana, were a series of heights, some 1,500 yards away, guarding access to the Nqutu plateau, itself split by deep ravines. The nearest heights – the iNyoni – rose several hundred feet above the plain. A spur, however, led up to the iNyoni from Isandlwana by way of the Tahelane ridge. To the east, out on the wide plain formed by the Nxbongo

river valley, lay the so-called Conical Kopje (known to the Zulu as Amatutshane), about a mile and half distant from the saddle or nek. The latter separated Isandlwana itself from another kopje to the south, Mahlabamkhosi, which became known as Black's or Stony Kopje. The plain itself stretched some four miles southwards towards the Malakatha mountain and Hlazakazi ridge and eight miles eastwards to the Magogo and Silutshana hills and Siphezi mountain.

It appeared to slope gently away from Isandlwana, but in reality, the plain was broken by the gullies known as dongas, notably the Mpofane and Nyogane, which ran roughly north to south. Thus many areas of dead ground, over which an enemy could approach without danger, obstructed the apparent open fields of fire for all that Chelmsford was to argue later that 'there never was a position where a small force could have made a better defensive stand'. Some have suggested that the terrain itself was an impediment to attack, but as the regimental history of the 24th later put it, to the Zulu, 'the rocky broken ground on the flanks was no more serious an obstacle than a ploughed field to our soldiers at home'.

Below: 'The 91st Regiment Leaving Camp at Durban for the Front': a contemporary engraving.

Stretching for some 1,300 yards, the camp was laid out along the eastern side of Isandlwana. The lines for the 2/3rd NNC were at the northernmost end, then those of the 1/3rd NNC, the 2/24th, Royal Artillery, and the colonial volunteers to the north of the track back to Rorke's Drift. The tents of the 1/24th were located just south of the track. The wagon park was located behind the tent lines with Chelmsford's headquarters' tents located behind the artillery park. Normally, the camp of the NNC would have been placed to the south in the delicately put language of Rothwell's official history for 'sanitary reasons' as this was downstream, but the nek was considered of 'such importance' that the 1/24th camp was placed there instead. Moreover, the northern flank close to the Nqutu plateau was 'regarded as less liable to any hostile attack'.

There appears to have been some difference of opinion on the merits or otherwise of the site, particularly when Chelmsford declined to laager the wagons as Glyn had suggested. Chelmsford remarked, 'It is not worth while, it will take too much time, and besides the wagons are most of them going back at once to Rorke's Drift for supplies.' Although strongly recommended to Chelmsford

prior to the campaign by a number of experienced Boer leaders, including the future President of the Transvaal, Paul Kruger, laagering was a hideously complicated business. It would have taken a considerable amount of time, especially as Chelmsford had not appointed an experienced 'laager commandant' in advance. Clery had subsequently failed to find a suitable civilian to take on the post. Moreover, it was intended to keep moving and those wagons not going on with the column would be used to bring up more supplies from Rorke's Drift. Thus Chelmsford was ignoring his own Field Force Regulations, which stated: 'Troops marching through the enemy's country, or where there is any possibility of attack, will, when halting, though but for a few hours, invariably form a wagon laager.' Against the Xhosa, however, it had also been the practice not to laager temporary camps while on the march. Interestingly, Chelmsford's own notes on the later findings of the Inquiry also stated that a laager was 'never intended to be used as a redoubt, but as protection for the oxen'. Indeed, at Centane, a laager had been used for precisely that purpose.

Entrenchment was an alternative. As already suggested, however, the camp extended across a frontage of at least 1,300 yards and it is not clear that entrenchments in themselves would have helped its defence. Clery later told the Inquiry that it was felt that the men were too exhausted to laager or otherwise entrench the camp by the time they reached it on the evening of 20 January. The ground was stony and entrenchment would have been a lengthy business. Chelmsford, therefore, was somewhat disingenuous in his later official report in suggesting that there were 'the materials for a hasty entrenchment which lay near to hand' for use on the morning of 22 January. He also later suggested that, if the tents had been lowered, they would have provided an additional impediment to the Zulu though this is doubtful.

Protection, it was assumed, would be the warning time provided by infantry pickets and mounted vedettes thrown forward of the camp, up to and including the Nqutu plateau, but not much beyond its edge in the iNyoni ridge. According to George Mansel of the Natal Mounted Police, he had originally posted his vedettes several miles out. Clery, however, had instructed him to draw them back much closer to the camp and, against Mansel's advice, to withdraw those to the rear of Isandlwana altogether, saying, 'My dear fellow, those vedettes are useless there, the rear always protects itself.' Crealock also rebuffed Mansel's colleague, Sub-Inspector F. L. Phillips, when he advised caution. Some care needs to be exercised with regard to Mansel's testimony, however, since his account was produced at the request of the family of Anthony Durnford, of whom much more will be said later. Of course, there were pickets and vedettes on the heights, albeit closer to the camp than Mansel believed necessary. As it happened, there was also a picket to the rear of Isandlwana on 22 January. Moreover, Mansel erred in implying that the Zulu were not concealed prior to the discovery of the main impi in the Ngwebeni valley on the morning of 22 January.

None the less, apart from Glyn, who was seen shaking his head at the position of the camp, other regulars also felt uneasy. The adjutant of the 1/24th, Lieutenant Teignmouth Melvill, expressed his fears of the camp's vulnerability to an unnamed officer: 'I know what you are thinking by your face, sir: you are abusing this camp and you are quite right! These Zulus will charge home,' and with our small numbers we ought to be in laager, or, at any rate, be prepared to stand shoulder to shoulder.' Melvill was somewhat unusual for the time, in having been commissioned directly from university without passing through the Royal Military College at Sandhurst. William Degacher also apparently favoured laagering the camp. Criticism was not welcomed, however, and all were aware of Crealock's scathing public rebuke to the experienced veteran of the Crimea and Mutiny, Major William Dunbar of the 2/24th, a few days earlier, when he had expressed fears about the safety of a temporary camp in the Batshe valley. If Dunbar was afraid to remain, Crealock had said, then 'we could send someone who was not'. Dunbar had immediately offered his resignation but had been persuaded to withdraw it. It would appear that Dunbar was also the 'field officer' who pointed out to a 'staff officer' the dangers of the broken ground in front of the camp and the need for a picket to the rear, only to be told, 'Well sir, if you are nervous we will put a picket of the [Natal Native] pioneers there.' Ironically, Dunbar was to be given command of the reconstituted 1/24th after Isandlwana.

There was no reason to suppose that the Zulu were likely to attack. Russell had led out a reconnaissance some 20 miles to the east of the Batshe towards Siphezi on 15 January and seen nothing. But reports were received of Zulu in the Mangeni gorge to the south, which contained the stronghold of 'Matyana' in the vicinity of Siphezi. This 'Matyana', actually Matshana kaSitshakuza of the Mchunu, is not to be confused with John Shepstone's old adversary, though both lived in the same area and British reports tend to speak of a campaign against the 'two Matyanas'. On 20 January Chelmsford himself had ridden out towards the Mangeni, into which fell a spectacular waterfall from the Hlazakazi, and resolved to send out a strong reconnaissance party that night. He did not apparently consult either Glyn or Clery, who were unaware of where the party was being sent or for what purpose.

Most of the two battalions of the 3rd NNC under the command of Lonsdale – only four companies remained in camp – and about 120 of the mounted police and volunteers under Dartnell started well before dawn on 21 January. While the NNC moved towards the Malakatha, the mounted troops moved towards the Hlazakazi. By mid-afternoon, the latter had encountered some 1,500 Zulu near

Below: 'South African Warfare, a halt of the 24th Regiment': local forces around the campfire on the right. An engraving by 'C.R.' after an eyewitness sketch by Melton Prior.

the Siphezi, who deployed threateningly in two horns. Zulu boys who had been taken prisoner during the course of the operation had also revealed that the main Zulu impi was to the north-east. Calling up Lonsdale's men to his assistance, Dartnell felt it unwise to proceed and, since it was now too late to do much more, decided to bivouac where he was on the northern slopes of the Hlazakazi. Dartnell sent a message back to Chelmsford by two of Chelmsford's ADCs who had accompanied him, Brevet Major Matthew Gosset and Captain Ernest Buller, that he would attack in the morning and required food and blankets for the Europeans. Subsequently, he dispatched a second message to Clery, which was taken by an officer named Davey, presumably the N. E. Davey who was acting as adjutant to the Natal volunteer corps as a whole, to the effect that, as the Zulu were in greater numbers than he had first thought, he needed at least two or three companies of the 24th as reinforcements before he could drive them off. Dartnell and Lonsdale, another former regular who had commanded Mfengu auxiliaries with great success against the Xhosa, were also concerned at the restlessness of the NNC. The night – spent in a hollow square formation – was to see a number of false alarms, in which at least some men slipped away.

At about 0130, Clery took the message to Glyn, but having been effectively supplanted by Chelmsford, Glyn simply referred Clery to the general. Clery roused Chelmsford: 'Lying on my face and hands close by his camp-bed I can still remember how I read from that crumpled piece of notebook paper written across in pencil, word after word that I had previously had such difficulty in deciphering in my own tent.' Dartnell had been expected to return to camp and Chelmsford later expressed himself 'much vexed' at Dartnell's disobedience of his orders. None the less, he decided to move out in Dartnell's support since the Mangeni was known to Fynn and others as a natural route frequented by *impi* in the past. Chelmsford also intended to select a new campsite in the valley.

The chosen elements, comprising six companies of the 2/24th, most of the mounted infantry and four guns moved out with Chelmsford at about 0330 on 22 January. With those already out with Dartnell and Lonsdale, Chelmsford would have some 2,500 men. In retrospect, many of those who survived by departing with Chelmsford recalled what Captain Henry Hallam-Parr characterised as the 'half-laughing condolences' on the part of those left behind in the camp. Hallam-Parr, who was Frere's Military Secretary but had managed to get himself attached unofficially to the staff of No 3 Column, also remembered his 'hurried and careless farewell' to Coghill and how his servant on bringing up his horse had said, 'I shall be here, sir, when you come back.' Charles Norris-Newman of the *London Standard*, who had been nicknamed 'Noggs' by Lonsdale, recalled: 'How well I remember that morning, and the dejected aspect of those officers belonging to the four companies of NNC detained by duty at the camp.' Lieutenant Henry Harford of the 99th Foot, attached to the 3rd NNC as Rupert Lonsdale's staff officer, remembered having noticed a strange 'more-or-less low-lying dark cloud' tinged by the rising sun over the camp, 'And there it hung for the best part of the morning, frowning as it were, over the fated Camp. I have never forgotten it.' Chelmsford's force moved out as silently as possible in light marching order without greatcoats, with one day's cooked rations and 70 rounds a man, thus not taking the additional 30 rounds usually issued in the likelihood of action.

Chelmsford reached Dartnell at about 0630, but the column was badly strung out behind him and at about 0930 he stopped for breakfast near the Magogo hill. While eating he received a message from the camp sent by Pulleine to Clery at 0805: 'Report just come in that the Zulus are advancing in force from the left front of the camp.' There was no urgency in the note, the force left behind seemed perfectly adequate and no one supposed that this could be the main Zulu army. Chelmsford, therefore, saw no reason to act on the note, remarking to Clery, 'There is nothing to be done on that,' but he did send his naval ADC, Lieutenant Berkeley Milne, to the top of the Magogo with his telescope to observe the distant camp, in company with Captain William Penn Symons of the 2/24th. Just as Smith-Dorrien was to figure in events in 1914 so, too, was Milne. By then Admiral Sir Berkeley Milne and commander-in-chief in the Mediterranean, he was instrumental in allowing two German warships, the *Goeben* and *Breslau*, to escape into Turkish waters in September 1914. Milne's companion on this occasion, Symons was to be killed as a Major-General not far from Isandlwana, commanding the British forces at Talana in the first major action of the South African War in October 1899.

Milne spent about an hour at his vantage point some twelve miles from the camp, but his view was partially impeded by the Silutshana. He could see no evidence of activity and the tents remained standing, but he did notice dark patches near to the camp, which he assumed to be oxen. Chelmsford saw no reason to alter his plans. Indeed, Captain Alan Gardner of the 14th Hussars, attached to the staff of No 3 Column, was sent back to Isandlwana between 1000 and 1100 with orders to Pulleine to strike camp and follow Chelmsford. Gardner subsequently suggested that it was intended to send on only the baggage of those troops out with Chelmsford and that Pulleine was to 'remain himself at his present camp and entrench it'. The order itself was lost in the fall of the camp and, since Gardner made no mention of his interpretation of the order at the Inquiry, it seems unlikely that Pulleine was intended to stay at Isandlwana. Gardner was accompanied by Major Stuart Smith of the Royal Artillery, four other officers, including the adjutant of the 2/24th, Lieutenant Henry Dyer, and a small escort of mounted infantry. After breakfast Chelmsford continued his advance.

When Chelmsford had first reached Dartnell, the Zulu encountered on the previous day had seemingly disappeared, but as the column was coming in Zulu appeared to the east. Soon Chelmsford's forward elements were in contact with the Zulu to their front on the Phindo and Silutshana heights, though the Zulu were gradually withdrawing north-eastwards towards the Siphezi. By this time most of Chelmsford's force was in the Nondweni valley, while he himself passed

Right: A Zulu warrior.
(National Army
Museum)

on to the Mangeni, where he intended to site the new camp. At about 1400 Chelmsford was found by Russell, who indicated that there was heavy firing close to the camp. Russell had seen an officer of the NNC – almost certainly Lieutenant B. Pohl – bearing a message from Hamilton-Browne that the main Zulu army was in close proximity to the camp about two hours earlier and had directed him to the rough whereabouts of the general. Apparently, he had not found Chelmsford or his staff. Subsequently Russell had received a second message from Hamilton-Browne, brought by a Sergeant Turner, that the camp was under attack. Russell had then sent Lieutenant H. A. Walsh of the Mounted Infantry and another officer named Davey, (possibly not the same man who had carried Dartnell's message to Chelmsford in the early hours of 22 January), to find his general. They, too, were unable to find him. Indeed, in a statement to the House of Lords in September 1880, Chelmsford admitted to having personally received only the first message from Pulleine. This was technically correct since, for example, the subsequent messages sent by Pulleine and Gardner were addressed to and received by Chelmsford's staff rather than Chelmsford himself at about 1500 when the party was on its way back to the camp.

Hamilton-Browne had been ordered to start his battalion back to the camp at about 0930. Not particularly known for his care of his native troops, Hamilton-Browne, according to his own account, uncharacteristically declined breakfast with Chelmsford and his staff on the grounds that his men had not eaten. He reflected later on the scene: 'I shall never forget the sight of that peaceful picnic. Here were the staff quietly breakfasting and the whole column scattered over the country!' His instructions were to clear ravines on the way back to camp in case, in Crealock's words, there were any Zulu 'hanging about near the camp'. When Hamilton-Browne asked what he should do if opposed, Crealock had told him, 'Oh, just brush them aside and go on.' At some point about this time, and presumably reflecting the early report received from Pulleine, according to Clery, Crealock dismissed the rumours, remarking 'How very amusing! Actually attacking our camp! Most amusing!' *En route* back to camp, Hamilton-Browne had taken two Zulu prisoners at about 1000 who revealed the presence of the main Zulu army in the vicinity. He had therefore sent Pohl back with this information.

Hamilton-Browne's spirits were now somewhat raised by coming across two men sent out from the camp to find him. They arrived with food and some bottles of whisky as an apology from Edgar Anstey and a fellow lieutenant of the 1/24th, Patrick Daly, for consuming the dinner prepared for Hamilton-Browne the night before when he had not returned to the camp. Later, at about 1100, Hamilton-Browne saw large numbers of Zulu between him and the camp and could see the bursting shells and the dark masses on the plateau. Hamilton-Browne then sent Turner with a message for Chelmsford: 'The Zulu army is attacking the left of the camp. The guns have opened up on them. The ground here is still suitable for guns and, mounted men. Will push on so as to act as support to them.' Getting closer, Hamilton-Browne observed the last stages of the battle for the camp through his field glasses, sending off yet another message which did not reach Chelmsford: 'The camp is being attacked on the left and in front, and as yet is holding its own. Ground still good for the rapid advance of guns and horses. Am moving forward as fast as I can.' His men now having only some fifteen rounds each, Hamilton-Browne retired to a rocky area sometime after 1300 and requested reinforcements, sending back a fourth message by one of his officers, Captain R. Develin, 'For God's sake come back, the camp is surrounded and must be taken unless helped.'

At about 1245, artillery firing was also heard by Harness, who was on the col between the Hlazakazi and the Magogo, and shells could be seen bursting on the plateau. Shortly afterwards he encountered Develin. Harness turned his four guns, and the two companies of the 2/24th escorting him, back towards the camp. Even at this late stage, Chelmsford's ADC, Gossett, who rode up at this time, is said to have exclaimed to Harness, 'It is all bosh, I do not hear big guns. You had better continue your march as ordered.' But other officers had also heard the guns and it would seem that a messenger from Durnford also reached Chelmsford's staff at about this time. At approximately 1315 Chelmsford himself went up to the Mdutshana hill with some of his staff. Nothing could be seen with any certainty, Charles Norris-Newman of the *London Standard*, writing: 'Every field glass was levelled at the camp. The sun was shining brightly on the white tents but all seemed quiet. No signs of firing or any engagement could be seen, and although bodies of men moving about could be distinguished, yet they were not unnaturally supposed to be our own troops.' Chelmsford did not believe the camp had fallen and Hamilton-Browne's message was not only thought to relate to the firing heard earlier, but also felt to be exaggerated, no one having much faith in Hamilton-Browne's judgement. Thus, Chelmsford, too, initially directed Harness to resume his march. Chelmsford, however, then decided to return himself to the camp with an escort at a somewhat leisurely pace. It is possible that this decision was taken sometime between 1400 and 1445. Clery subsequently suggested it was much later and, conceivably, it was in response to the messages from Pulleine and Gardner received at about 1500, of which more later. Eventually, Chelmsford reached Hamilton-Browne's position at about 1530, still some five miles short of Isandlwana.

According to Hamilton-Browne, when he finally met Chelmsford to tell him the camp had fallen, Chelmsford replied, 'How dare you tell me such a falsehood? Get your men into line at once and advance.' Known as 'Maori' Browne, Hamilton-Browne claimed considerable fighting experience in the Maori Wars in New Zealand, but he was considered little more than an adventurer. Indeed, his various published reminiscences were heavily fictionalised. He claimed to have fought in New Zealand from 1866–71, but the authorities there later rejected his claims to the New Zealand Medal and a pension. It was discovered that he had only served in the Armed Constabulary from 1872–75 after the end of hostilities against the Maori. His claims to have been a Papal Zouave and to have fought

Indians in the USA were equally suspect, although he had certainly served with the irregulars in the Ninth Frontier War. The irony, of course, is that on this occasion he was telling the truth.

Not long after Chelmsford had joined Hamilton-Browne, Lonsdale struggled in with dire news. Feeling ill, Lonsdale, who had suffered a bad fall from his horse earlier in January, had ridden back to the camp to arrange for supplies to be sent out for his battalion. Taking little notice of his surroundings, he had ridden into the outskirts of the camp sometime between 1400 and 1430 without initially noticing that the Zulu were in possession of it. Indeed, he even dismissed some shots aimed at him as a mistake by some member of the NNC. Suddenly confronted by a Zulu with a blood-tipped assegai, he was jolted into consciousness and spurred his tired pony, Dot, into life. In his often quoted account, Lonsdale wrote: 'I shall never close my eyes in sleep again without seeing that yelling horde of Zulus rushing after me, brandishing their bloody spears and wondering whether my poor horse had steam enough left in him to carry me out of their reach.' In utter disbelief, Chelmsford is said to have exclaimed of Lonsdale's news, 'But I left over 1,000 men to guard the camp.'

It took until 1800 for Chelmsford to concentrate his exhausted force – Glyn and his men had had to cover 7½ miles in two hours – and it was not until 2100, two hours after sunset, that he regained the saddle, Wilsone Black having seized Mahlabamkhosi, which thus became known as Black's Kopje. Only then did the full extent of the catastrophe become apparent. According to Clery, Chelmsford could not conceal a 'look of gloom and pain' but had the presence of mind to rouse the 2/24th to action: 'Men, the enemy has taken our camp. Many of our friends must have lost their lives in defending it. There is nothing left for us now but to fight our way through – and mind, we must fight hard, for we will have to fight for our lives. I know you and I know I can depend on you.' Famously, firing could be heard in the direction of Rorke's Drift and the shape of the Oskarberg mountain near the drift was illuminated by the red glare of the mission station in flames.

Chelmsford's men took what rest they could amid the detritus of the camp, a number finding in the morning that they had slept on the dead. The most horrifying aspect for the British was the ritual disembowelling (qaqa) of their erstwhile comrades, the Zulu believing that it was necessary to slit open a slain enemy's stomach to allow the spirit to escape, lest the victim haunt his slayer. While some reports may have been exaggerated, it is clear that further mutilation was inflicted on bodies in many cases, with some body parts being used for the preparation of ritual medicines (intelezi). Facial hair seems to have been especially prized and a number of bearded jawbones were certainly disarticulated. Another part of Zulu ritual was to stab a corpse to denote participation in the kill, this 'washing of the spears' extending to those who had not done the actual killing but who could be deemed to have shared in it by their presence. At the same time, it was also a mark of honour to the dead since the Zulu reserved such post-mortem stabbing for the most dangerous prey in hunting such as lion. The stripping of the dead was also common since the wearing of an enemy's clothes was considered beneficial to the slayer's subsequent purification.

The camp, of course, had also been thoroughly looted by the Zulu, anything valued by the Zulu such as rifles, blankets and oxen carried off, though many oxen were killed in the frenzy of bloodlust that followed the fall of the camp. A few horses were taken but most were killed because the Zulu believed them 'the feet of the white men'. Pets, too, were killed: some escaped and turned up in later days, while some dogs that survived formed packs that subsequently ravaged the corpses. As a Zulu boy who visited the battlefield shortly after the action recalled in 1884: 'Dead was the horse, dead too, the mule, dead was the dog, dead was the monkey, dead were the wagons, dead were the tents, dead were the boxes, dead was everything, even to the very metals.' In some cases, plundering had dire consequences for the Zulu were so thirsty after the battle that they consumed any liquid they could find including ink and even paraffin. About 800 Martin-Henry rifles and an estimated 40,000 cartridges had been taken.

Writing to his father, Sergeant Warren of N Battery, who had been out with Harness, '... could not help crying to see how the poor fellows were massacred. They were first shot and then assegaied, the Zulus mutilated them and stuck them with the assegai all over the body.' Similarly, Patrick Farrell of the 2/24th wrote to his brother, 'It was enough to make your blood run cold to see the white men cut open, worst than ever was done in the Indian Mutiny.' James Cook of the 2/24th wrote, 'The sight at the camp was horrible. Every white man that was killed or wounded was ripped up, and their bowels torn out; so there was no chance of anyone being left alive on the field.' A correspondent of the *Natal Mercury* remembered the night spent on the field: 'Oh! How dreadful to all were those fearful hours which followed when all of us had to wait with what patience we could for daybreak, knowing that we were standing and lying among the bodies of our own comrades, though how many we little knew then. Many and deep were the sobs which came from the breasts of those who, may be, never sobbed before, at discovering, even in the dim morning light, the bodies of dear friends brutally massacred, stripped of all clothing, disembowelled, and in some cases with their heads cut off. How that night passed, I fancy few of us knew ...'

Small wonder that Chelmsford moved his column off towards Rorke's Drift as early as possible before the full light of day unnerved his men. Chelmsford wrote to the Duke of Cambridge, Commander-in-Chief at the War Office, that he felt unable to pause to bury the dead. To do so '... partially could only have the effect of bringing home to the troops the full extent of the disaster, of which they were to a certain extent kept in ignorance owing to the darkness'. Moving off, his force passed a large body of Zulu returning up the Batshe valley – those who had attacked Rorke's Drift – but both sides were too exhausted to fight after their exertions of the previous day. Chelmsford's column reached Rorke's Drift at about 0800 on 23 January, much relieved to find the post had held out.

4

THE BATTLE FOR THE CAMP

At Isandlwana itself, command had devolved upon Pulleine of the 1/24th. Aged 40, and short in stature, the popular Pulleine had seen no combat, having served in staff appointments during the Ninth Frontier War, though he had also raised a unit of irregulars popularly known as 'Pulleine's Lambs'. He had rejoined the battalion only on 17 January from duties with the Remount Department in Pietermaritzburg. Pulleine had five companies of his own regiment – A, C, E, F and H, commanded respectively by Lieutenant Francis Porteous, Captain Reginald Younghusband, Lieutenant Charles Cavaye, Captain William Mostyn, and Captain George Wardell – plus G Company of the 2/24th under Lieutenant Charles Pope. It is sometimes suggested that Cavaye commanded A Company and Porteous E Company, but this is erroneous. With Pulleine commanding the camp, overall command of the 1/24th companies devolved to William Degacher as acting Major. In addition there were two guns of N Battery, 5th Brigade Royal Artillery; various elements of the 1st Squadron, Imperial Mounted Infantry; colonials from the Natal Mounted Police, Newcastle Mounted Rifles, Buffalo Border Guard and Natal Carbineers; various camp casuals and assorted staff; and four companies of the NNC. The latter comprised Nos. 4 and 5 Companies of the 2/3rd (under Captains Edward Erskine and A. T. Barry) and Nos. 6 and 9 Companies of the 1/3rd (under Captains R. Krohn and James Lonsdale). Mostyn's company had only marched into the camp from Helpmekaar on 20 January while Pope's company was left in camp as it was scheduled for picket duty on the 22nd. In all, this comprised about 1,170 men, of whom approximately 750 were Europeans, and 597 regulars.

Below:
Lieutenant-General
Lord Chelmsford.
(I. Beckett)

Clery later wrote to a friend, Colonel George Harman, that, at the last minute and on his own initiative since he realised nothing had been done, he had left orders for Pulleine. These were to assume command of the camp, to draw in the infantry pickets closer to the camp, but to keep out the mounted vedettes, and to have a wagon available to be sent forward with ammunition to support Chelmsford if necessary. Just before leaving camp, Clery saw Pulleine to confirm the orders. Only belatedly did Chelmsford realise that he had not left any orders for Pulleine and was relieved to find that Clery had done so. Reporting to Frere after the disaster, Hallam-Parr suggested that, if attacked, Pulleine's orders were to 'strike camp, contract his lines and act steadily on the defensive'. While it has been suggested that this meant laagering, it would appear more likely that this was merely Hallam-Parr's précis of Clery's orders to Pulleine, striking the camp referring merely to pulling down the tents. It has also been suggested that Clery may not have left any orders in writing, especially since Durnford's staff officer, Lieutenant William Cochrane of the 32nd Foot, mentioned that Pulleine only informed Durnford of his 'verbal orders' when Durnford reached Isandlwana on 22 January. Clery, however, had little reason to support the later version of events put out by Chelmsford and Crealock.

Mounted pickets of the Natal Carbineers out on Qwabe hill across the plain beyond the Conical Kopje, and on the Nyezi feature, another two miles or so beyond that, both reported Zulu approaching from the north-east at about 0800, resulting in Pulleine sending his first message to Chelmsford. The defenders were drawn out on the eastern side of the camp inclined towards the iNyoni. The oxen were also brought in closer to the wagons, while a messenger was sent to bring in a party of the 1/24th under Lieutenant Edgar Anstey of F Company employed on improving the road back to Rorke's Drift. Some 40 or so wagons, which had been intended to start back to Rorke's Drift, remained at the rear of the camp, their oxen yoked, to await a safer moment to start. At the same time, some other wagons at least were inspanned. At about 0900, a few Zulu appeared on the plateau but soon disappeared. It was reported that some were retiring to the north-east but others moving to the north-west. During the Ninth Frontier War, large groups of the enemy had often been seen without anything subsequently developing and no alarm was felt at the sightings for, as Lieutenant Henry Curling of N5 Battery was to write later, no one 'dreamed they would come on'.

Sometime between 1000 and 1030, Durnford arrived with some 450 men from No 2 Column, Pulleine having been told to expect his arrival. Durnford's column principally comprised the five troops of the Natal Native Horse under Captain William Barton; and two amaNgwane companies of the 1/1st NNC under Captains Walter Stafford and Charles Nourse. In addition, there was No 11 Rocket Battery, 7th Brigade, Royal Artillery under Major Francis Russell, which was actually mostly manned by privates drawn from the 24th.

Through a combination of his estrangement from his wife and his own gambling, Durnford, who was aged 48 in 1879, had been forced into a succession of overseas postings. He had arrived in South Africa in 1872 and acted as Colonial Engineer from 1873–75. Durnford had attended Cetshwayo's coronation and, in November 1873, had led an expedition of colonial volunteers to put down the rebellion of Langalibalele, only to see his force put to flight at Bushman's Pass. It had been a small-scale but embarrassing affair. Five of Durnford's men were killed and he received an assegai thrust through his left elbow, which shattered the nerve and left his arm crippled for life. Subsequently, Langalibalele was betrayed and apprehended by the Cape Frontier Police. Durnford's courage during the retreat was widely recognised, but the expedition raised questions as to his abilities in command. Moreover, his advocacy of the rights of the Phutile, a tribe wrongly accused of conspiring with Langalibalele, made Durnford unpopular with the colonists, as did his friendship with the Colenso family. He left Natal in May 1876, but, finding service in Ireland uncongenial, returned to his former post of Colonial Engineer in early 1877, sitting, as already related, on the disputed territory commission.

Durnford had long been an advocate of using local African forces and, as suggested previously, was instrumental in persuading Chelmsford to raise the NNC

Below: Frontier Light Horse: a contemporary engraving.

and the Natal Native Pioneers. He was given No 2 Column, with the 1st NNC under his direct command, as well as the Natal Native Horse. With the changes to Chelmsford's original plans, No 2 Column was tasked only with the defence of the border. It is clear, however, that Chelmsford was wary of Durnford's supposed recklessness. Indeed, Durnford had moved his column down to the Tugela in response to a rumour about Zulu movements circulated by Bishop Hans Schreuder, a leading Norwegian missionary based at Eshowe. He was sharply ordered back by Chelmsford, who threatened to remove him from command though Durnford was later ordered up to Rorke's Drift with his horsemen and Major Harcourt Bengough's 2/1st NNC. Ultimately, it would appear that Chelmsford intended Durnford to come under Pearson's command though continuing to act separately. Durnford was especially depressed at being left behind, writing to his mother, 'I have no news, am stupid and dull, and "down", so adieu

Below: A reconnaissance party of British lancers and local forces: a contemporary engraving.

for the day.' At about 0200 on 21 January, Chelmsford ordered Durnford up to Isandlwana with the force immediately at his disposal, with Bengough's men – still back at Sandspruit – to move towards the Mangeni. The remainder of the 1/1st NNC and the 3/1st NNC were still at the Middle Drift.

Chelmsford's order was brought to Durnford by the transport officer with No 3 Column, Lieutenant Horace Smith-Dorrien of the 95th Foot, who rode back down to Rorke's Drift to find him. Smith-Dorrien reached Rorke's Drift at about 0600 but Durnford was out on a mission to try and acquire more wagons from the local Boers and one of Durnford's officers, Lieutenant Alfred Henderson of the Hlubi Troop, was sent off to bring him back. Smith-Dorrien rode back to the camp at about 0800, having borrowed some cartridges for his revolver from Bromhead. He had ridden down to the drift 'entirely alone' and through country that was 'wild and new to me' without any ammunition.

Lieutenant John Chard of the Royal Engineers, too, rode up to the camp from Rorke's Drift early that morning, to clarify orders received. These had directed him to send up some of his engineers from Rorke's Drift, where he was overseeing the punts used to ferry men and supplies across the Buffalo. Chard arrived at the camp just before Durnford, five men following with a wagon carrying their equipment. By this time, of course, Zulu had been seen on the plateau. Worried that the punts might be at risk from a 'dash at the drift', Chard left four of his men to continue to the camp and returned to Rorke's Drift with the other, his batman Driver Edward Robson. Chard passed Durnford and his men on the track behind the mountain. While Chard rode back to his date with destiny, his four men were all to perish.

Chelmsford had originally told Clery to order up Durnford at the same time that preparations were being made for the march to reinforce Dartnell and Lonsdale. Crealock had intervened to point out that Durnford was not under Glyn but held an independent command, requiring orders from Chelmsford. Not only had Pulleine's orders been issued hastily but it was also the case that Chelmsford had not left any precise indication of who was to command once Durnford, four years senior to Pulleine, arrived. In fact, Durnford had been promoted to Brevet Colonel in December but the news had yet to reach South Africa. Crealock claimed that Durnford had been ordered to take command and Cochrane certainly stated at the Inquiry that Durnford did so, and reiterated the point in his subsequent official report. Crealock later also suggested that the orders

Clery had issued to Pulleine to defend the camp were effectively binding upon Durnford. Crealock's actual instructions to Durnford, however, were later found in Crealock's notebook recovered from the battlefield of Isandlwana: they merely ordered Durnford up to the camp without any precise instructions either to reinforce it or, indeed, to assume command. Crealock, therefore, knowingly lied. Moreover, it might be argued that since which 'camp' was not specified, Durnford might have legitimately interpreted this to mean the new camp Chelmsford intended to establish in the Mangeni. Certainly, the orders issued to Durnford on 19 January directing him up to Rorke's Drift had specified that he should co-operate with No 3 Column 'in clearing the country occupied by the chief Matyana'. In that sense, Durnford carried out the orders sent to him by Chelmsford.

Aware of the reports of a Zulu presence, but unclear as to the precise situation from a confused report brought in from the Nqutu plateau at about this time

Below: Chelmsford's Orders to Durnford on 19 January 1879, a copy later recovered from the battleflield of Isandlwana. (National Army Museum)

by Lieutenant Walter Higginson of the 1/3rd NNC, Durnford sent some men up to the top of Isandlwana. They could see nothing. Durnford then indicated that he would not stay in the camp but head off any possible Zulu attempt to get behind Chelmsford since the reports seemed to suggest that the Zulu were retiring in that direction. According to Cochrane, Durnford asked Pulleine for two companies of the 24th but Pulleine declined on the grounds that his orders were to defend the camp. Durnford contested the point and Pulleine is said to have remarked, 'Oh, very well; of course if you order them I'll give you them.' The statement of an unnamed native wagon driver recorded later by Chelmsford's interpreters, Drummond and Henry Longcast, somewhat improbably stated that he had witnessed the difference of opinion between Durnford and Pulleine. At an even greater distance in time from the event, Stafford of the NNC also recalled an argument when writing in 1938. Cochrane, however, reported the exchanges as being 'perfectly genial and courteous'. At this point Pulleine consulted his officers and Melvill told Durnford, 'Colonel, I really do not think Colonel Pulleine would be doing right to send any men out of camp when his orders are to "defend the camp".' Acquiescing, Durnford remarked, according to Cochrane's later report, 'Very well, perhaps I had better not take them. I will go with my own men.' None the less, Durnford pointedly remarked, 'If you see us in difficulties you must send and support us'. Again, according to Cochrane, Pulleine agreed to do so.

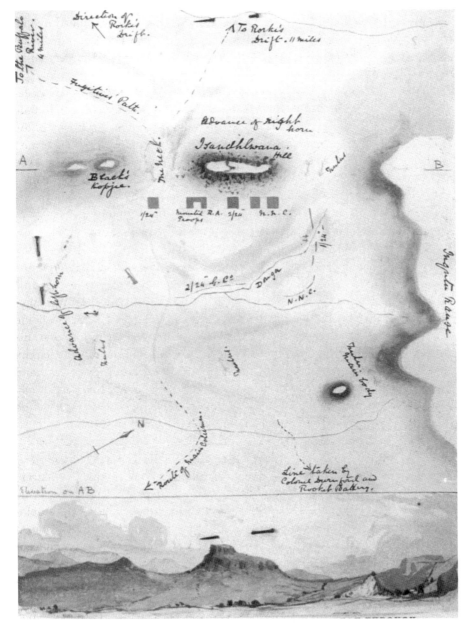

Left: A map of Isandlwana compiled by Captain William Penn Symons of the 24th Foot for his regimental account of the battle. As a major-general, Symons was to be killed at Talana, only some 50 kms from Isandlwana, in the first engagement of the South African War in October 1899. (National Army Museum)

After a hurried breakfast – Durnford remained standing throughout – since they had left Rorke's Drift without eating, Durnford's men moved off some time between 1030 and 1100. Captains George Shepstone – yet another of Theophilus Shepstone's sons, acting as Durnford's political officer – and William Barton accompanied two of the Sikali troops of the Natal Native Horse – together 107 strong – under Lieutenants Charles Raw and Joseph Roberts, which moved up towards the Nqutu plateau. A little later at about 1115, Durnford himself headed across the plain with the Edendale and Hlubi troops under Lieutenants Harry Davies and Alfred Henderson respectively, amounting to 102 men. They were trailed at about 1130 by Major Russell's three rocket battery troughs carried on mules some two miles behind with Nourse's NNC (amaNgwane) company as escort. Stafford's NNC company (also amaNgwane) was still coming into the camp with Durnford's wagons and Durnford, having received reports that some Zulu were moving towards the rear of the camp, sent back his remaining mounted troop of Sikali Horse – some 50 men – under Lieutenant Richard Wyatt Vause to see Stafford safely in. At about the same time, Cavaye's E Company was sent up on to the Tahelane ridge about 1,200 yards from the camp to reinforce and replace the pickets from the NNC, who moved forward after Roberts and Raw.

Relying on a particular interpretation of the testimony of Captain Edward Essex of the 75th Foot, the director of transport for No 3 Column, Chelmsford later argued that Cavaye was sent out at Durnford's request. Certainly, it would appear that the move was more in accordance with Pulleine's desire to support Durnford than his instructions to defend the camp. The remaining men in the camp, according to a written submission to the Inquiry by Essex, marched 'to their private parades' though they were expected to remain in readiness. Since breakfast had been abandoned at the time of the first stand-to at 0800, an early lunch was now taken.

Up on the plateau, Roberts moved to the north while Raw went eastwards. Sometime between 1115 and 1145, some of Raw's men saw and gave chase to some Zulu herding a few cattle. Riding up to a crest of the Ngwebeni valley known as Mabaso, and, in one of the most dramatic incidents of the battle, they suddenly came across the Zulu army. Once discovered, the entire army rose. The astonished patrol dismounted and fired one volley before hastily retiring. Less dramatically, Raw himself merely reported later that, as his men followed up groups of Zulu, the whole *impi* showed 'itself from behind a hill in front where they had evidently been waiting'. Retiring steadily, Raw encountered Shepstone, who at once sent off some men to warn Durnford out on the plain and returned himself to the camp to warn Pulleine. Lieutenant Durrant Scott on vedette duty at the Conical Kopje, and whose men had already been engaged with some of the Zulu groups observed earlier, also sent two Natal Carbineers to warn Durnford. It is possible that they reached him before Shepstone's messengers. Told that he was in danger of being cut off, according to Harry Davies, Durnford replied, 'The enemy can't surround us, and if they do, we will cut our way through them.' He also peremptorily ordered Scott's Carbineers to support his force when they indicated that Scott's orders from Pulleine were to remain on the Conical Kopje.

Out on the plain, Russell ignored the advice of two more of Scott's Carbineers, who rode by on their way back to Scott's position from observing the Zulu on the plateau, and pressed on. Hearing the firing up on the plateau, Russell moved off to the left to ascend. His rocket battery was overwhelmed by the iNgobamakhosi about two or three miles from the camp some way beyond the Conical Kopje, possibly *en route* to the plateau by way of a feature known as the 'Notch' to the left of a higher feature known as Itusi. Russell's three rocket troughs were

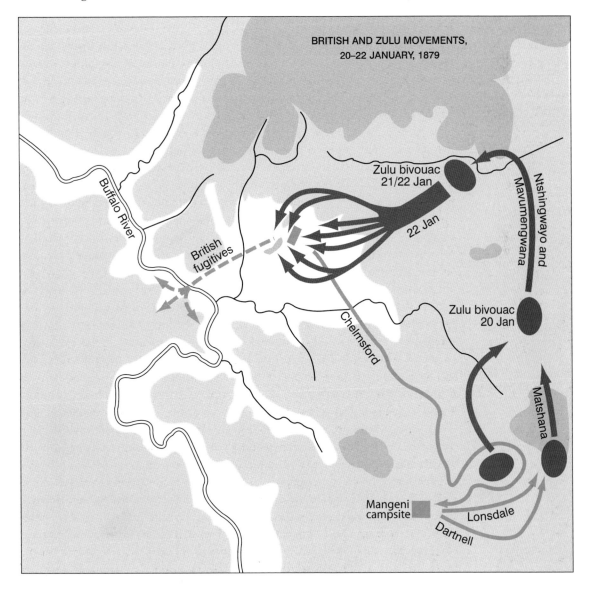

BRITISH AND ZULU MOVEMENTS,
20–22 JANUARY, 1879

Buffalo River

British fugitives

Zulu bivouac
21/22 Jan

22 Jan

Ntshingwayo and
Mavumengwana

Zulu bivouac
20 Jan

Chelmsford

Matshana

Mangeni
campsite

Lonsdale

Dartnell

mounted on mules and he managed to get off only one rocket. In any case the Hale's rocket, a 9-pounder weapon with a range of 1,300 yards, was more notable for the supposed psychological effect of its noise than its likely impact as a munition. Russell and five of his eight men were shot down, the other three – Privates Grant, Johnson and Trainer – managing to get away. The battery's mules scattered and Nourse's company disintegrated, Nourse simply reporting to the Inquiry that 'we retired on to the camp as well as we could'. Well ahead of the rocket battery, in fact, possibly as much as four or five miles from the camp, Durnford was confronted with large numbers of Zulu from the iNgobamakhosi and uMbonambi ('Seers of Evil') to his front. He retreated to the Nyanga donga, where he was reinforced by some of the Natal Carbineers, who had been on the Conical Kopje. Retiring steadily, they came across the remnant of the rocket battery and Nourse and five of his men, collecting them as they went. Durnford continued his retreat to another donga – the Nyogane –about a mile from the camp. Durnford appears to have sent some of his men to warn Chelmsford and, though they were seen by a number of Chelmsford's command at various stages in the afternoon, no one seems to have taken their reports seriously.

According to Jabez Molife of Henderson's Troop, Durnford's retreat was methodical: 'After this we remounted and retreated 20 yards, always in a long thin line, then dismounted and fired, up again for another ten yards, dismounted and fired again, and so on ten yards at a time, firing always, slowly back towards the camp.' Once at the donga, again according to Molife, Durnford 'rode up and down our line continually, encouraging us all; he was very calm & cheerful talking & even laughing with us. "Fire! My boys", "Well done, my boys!" he cried'. If his men had trouble extracting cartridges from their carbines, Durnford dismounted and 'taking the gun between his knees, because of only having only one hand with strength in it, he pulled the cartridge out & gave back the gun'. It has been argued that Durnford probably remained at the Nyogane donga, thus contributing to the over-extension of the defensive line, because his men's horses were blown after their exertions. They had been almost constantly on the move since they had left Rorke's Drift between 0730 and 0800. One of the sons of Sihayo, whose action had been the pretext for war, Mehlokazulu, was serving with the iNgobamakhosi opposite Durnford's position. He left a description of Durnford's action: 'They had drawn their horses into this donga, and all we could see were the helmets. They fired so heavily we had to retire; we kept lying down and rising again … Then, when the firing became very heavy – too hot – we retired towards the left wing, towards Rorke's Drift, and they then withdrew.'

The Zulu army encountered by Raw's men was led by Ntshingwayo kaMahole of the Khoza, who was almost 70, and the 45-year-old Mavumengwana kaNdela of the Ntuli. It was some 20,000–24,000 strong. Five months later, the route of the *impi* was still apparent from the grass trampled by its single great column. Ntshingwayo was second only to Mnyamana on the council, having been a respected councillor to Mpande. He was also renowned as an orator, taking a prominent part in the ceremonial declaiming of praise-poems on national occasions. The son of one of Dingane's principal commanders, Mavumengwana was a senior *induna* of the uThulwana and a close friend of Cetshwayo. Mavumengwana's brother was also leading the force sent to confront Pearson's column. At Isandlwana, the intended composition of the *impi*'s horns and chest became totally disrupted by the suddenness with which the action was brought on, the original left horn becoming the right, the right the centre, and the centre the left.

During the action, therefore, the right horn consisted of the uDududu ('The Contemptibles'), iSangqu ('The White Tails'), and iMbube ('Lion') regiments of the uNodwengu corps, and the uNokhenke ('The Dividers') of the iKhanda corps. The centre comprised the umCijo ('The Sharp Pointed'), who were also known as the uKhandempemvu; some of the uMxhapho ('The Sprinklers'); and the uMbonambi, though the latter seem to have ended up with the left horn. The left horn itself initially comprised the iNgobamakhosi and uVe ('The Fly-catcher Bird'). Most of these regiments in the horns and chest were younger unmarried men. The reserve uNdi corps of mostly older married regiments comprised the uThulwana, iNdluyengwe ('The Leopard's Beauty Spots'), uDloko ('Snake') and iNdlondlo ('Euphorbia Tree') regiments under the command of Dabulamanzi kaMpande. Dabulamanzi was Cetshwayo's younger brother, memorably described by Donald Morris as a 'roistering fighter now in his dissolute prime'. Two other brothers of the King, Magwende kaMpande and Ndabuko kaMpande, were also present as well as Cetshwayo's cousin, the influential Zibhebhu, who commanded the uDloko and was responsible for directing the *impi*'s scouts on the campaign. It is possible that some additional Zulu regiments were represented at Isandlwana by elements incorporated in others, such as men of the uMtulisazwi included in the umCijo and men of the Nkonkone included in the uThulwana. Similarly, it has also been suggested that elements of the umHlanga and unQakamatye served with the umCijo, and of the umSikaba with the uNodwengu corps.

The *impi* had left Ulundi on 17 January and, by short marches, had reached Siphezi on the 20th. Apparently there was some disagreement with Matshana on the best approach to the British camp. Matshana was not altogether trusted by the other senior Zulu commanders because he was a 'Natal Kaffir', who had settled in Zululand in 1858 and become a royal favourite. Indeed the British thought that Matshana might come over to them, the possibility encouraging Chelmsford's moves towards the Mangeni rather than the direct route to Ulundi by way of Siphezi. In the event, the *impi* moved westwards in small groups to the Ngwebeni valley, some four or five miles north-east of Isandlwana, on 21 January with the intention of working their way around the rear of the British column while Matshana continued to operate near the Mangeni. The *impi* had passed Dartnell going in the opposite direction undetected though one of the Zulu flanking parties had been spotted by Dartnell. No fires were lit in the Ngwebeni and the Zulu remained concealed though Scott's vedettes had observed the movement of some of the groups still making their way towards the Ngwebeni, which had prompted the first stand-to in the camp. In fact the Natal Carbineers did become engaged with some of these groups at about 0700.

It was in the Ngwebeni, however, that the main *impi* was then discovered by Raw, groups having been sent out to bring in food and cattle. Since 22/23 January marked a new moon, when the omens would be more propitious, Evelyn Wood later suggested that the original intention of the Zulu was to fall on the rear of the camp on 23 January. The Zulu themselves suggested that they would not have attacked on 22 January unless discovered. It is equally possible, however, that the Zulu intended to attack later on 22 January. Of course the Zulu later stressed that there was no intention of fighting on a day so inauspicious as that of the 'dead moon', but this did not prevent Matshana's followers continuing the engagement with Chelmsford on that very day. Moreover, the Zulu also attacked Pearson's column at Nyezane on 22 January. John Laband, therefore, has argued, in view of an impending conference of Zulu commanders, that the Zulu may well have intended to attack the camp later on 22 January. Thus Raw's men stumbling on the *impi* merely accelerated events.

It remains a matter of debate whether Chelmsford was deliberately lured into splitting his force by Matshana who may thus have staged some kind of deliberate diversion, as opposed to being simply persuaded by the other Zulu not to accompany them to the Ngwebeni. In fact, Matshana himself was on his way to meet the other Zulu commanders in the Ngwebeni on 21 January when he was chased by one of Dartnell's patrols. It is certainly possible that the fires the Zulu lit on the hills around Dartnell's position on the night of 21 January were intended both to mask the movement of the main *impi* to the Ngwebeni and to enable Matshana to withdraw his warriors. In that sense, they were a decoy, but the Zulu cannot have anticipated that Chelmsford would necessarily have split his force in response to Dartnell's encounter. Cetshwayo later claimed that Ntshingwayo had been instructed to send a peace delegation to Chelmsford before attacking and that his commanders were still debating whom to send when the discovery of the *impi* triggered the battle. This seems unlikely though there is no doubt that Cetshwayo had sent a number of emissaries to the British prior to the expiry of the ultimatum. Isandlwana made any negotiated settlement all but impossible, though this did not prevent Cetshwayo dispatching more peace emissaries in March, May, and June 1879.

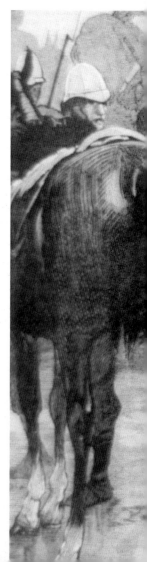

It was the umCijo who apparently reacted first to the appearance of Raw's men, provoked by the volley fired at them. As already indicated, the sudden occurrence disrupted the intended Zulu organisation, and there was no time for the usual practice of last-minute purification rituals and gathering round the commander in a circle to listen to his final instructions. Indeed, the *izinduna* desperately tried to bring some order to the advance. The right horn and centre moved across the plateau while the left horn moved down towards the Conical Kopje, but with the right wing and centre far ahead of the left. In the event, the uDududu, iMbube and iSangqu did not come down on to the plain but continued across the plateau until they were behind Isandlwana. Subsequently, they came down to cut off the British rear. So it was the uNokhenke, which did move down to the plain, together with the centre and left wing that took the brunt of the battle. At least the reserve was successfully held back, though some broke away to join the battle, the regiments being formed in the customary circle with their backs to the enemy to be given their instructions and ritually doctored for

Below: A stand-to before dawn at Landman's Drift: an engraving by W. J. Palmer after R. Caton Woodville, based upon an eyewitness sketch by Melton Prior.

action. The reserve then moved across the plateau behind Isandlwana to inter-
cept the main track back to Rorke's Drift, Dabulamanzi subsequently sending
the iNdluyengwe to attack the survivors fleeing down towards the Buffalo.

It was the uNdi corps that was to make the subsequent attack on Rorke's Drift,
Dabulamanzi being somewhat ambitious and his regiments, notably the
uThulwana, anxious to gain some kudos for themselves, especially given the
prominence of the rival iNgobamakhosi in the battle they had missed. It would
appear that, initially, the Zulu had intended merely a limited incursion to burn

Right: The
controversial Colonel
Anthony Durnford, a
convenient scapegoat
for Chelmsford and
his staff after his
death at Isandlwana.
(National Army
Museum)

farms and lift cattle and then happened upon what appeared to be an easy tempting target of a supply post defended by only a few redcoats. Indeed, some of the uNdi corps were not at Rorke's Drift, but pursuing plunder in the direction of Helpmekaar. Cetshwayo was reportedly extremely angry that his orders not to enter Natal had been ignored.

In the camp, a new stand-to was ordered at about 1200 as Shepstone rode in to warn of the Zulu advance, Mostyn's F Company having been sent out to reinforce Cavaye's E Company when firing was heard from the plateau. Essex, who had gone up to see what was happening, carried a message to Cavaye from Mostyn that he was moving up to his support. Essex had been writing in his tent, and was supremely unconcerned: 'I had my [field] glasses over my shoulder and thought I might as well take my revolver; but did not trouble to put on my sword, as I thought nothing of the matter and expected to be back in half an hour to complete my letters.' Barry's NNC company – amaChunu – originally on picket duty on the prominent knoll known as the Magogo, and then sent forward after Raw and Roberts, however, had already broken and run. Essex also saw some of the Natal Native Horse retiring though he saw other NNC men to the right who may have been from Erskine's Company – amaChunu like those of Barry. On reaching Cavaye, Essex found them deployed in extended order and firing at Zulu of the uNokenke and the uDududu, who were about 800 yards away and moving across Cavaye's front towards the rear of Isandlwana. Essex noted that Cavaye had sent a section under Second Lieutenant Edward Dyson some 500 yards to the left and Mostyn moved his company into the gap between Cavaye and Dyson. Mostyn and Cavaye were deployed in a shallow valley beyond the crest of the Tahelane and, therefore, not visible from the camp. Essex mentioned native infantry being off to the right of Cavaye's position but did not identify them further. They may have been remnants of Barry's company or possibly that of Edward Erskine.

Dyson's section appears to have been overwhelmed at a very early stage. Indeed, Chelmsford's later report that one company 'went off to the extreme left and has never been heard of since' may well be a reference to Dyson. It has also been argued that the Martini-Henry rifles undoubtedly used by the Zulu at Rorke's Drift probably came from Dyson's section, annihilated by the uNdi corps as it swept over the plateau. Indeed, when the main camp area was fenced off in 1928, other burial cairns were subsequently lost. Some cairns, however, were rediscovered on the plateau in 1958, suggesting that Dyson was overwhelmed there; since then the cairns have once more been lost to the processes of time. A small party of engineers repairing the road to Rorke's Drift was also overwhelmed by the uNdi corps en route to the outpost.

Shortly after Mostyn's arrival to reinforce Cavaye, Melvill sent a message up to Essex to order the line to fall back slowly as Zulu were now appearing in the rear of the camp. Essex timed the withdrawal at about 1230, but attention has been drawn by Edmund Yorke to what appears to be a recently discovered written message from Pulleine to Cavaye sent at 1130, directing him to retire on the camp: 'Zulus are advancing on your right in force. Retire on camp in order. E Company will support your right. NNC on your left.' E Company, of course, was Cavaye's own and Yorke attributes this to confusion on Pulleine's part. Either in receipt of Pulleine's order or Essex's verbal message, the men did withdraw from the Tahelane ridge apparently in some confusion, but they were soon reorganised, Cavaye and Mostyn drawing up their companies at the foot of the plateau. Possibly they drew in some of Barry's remaining men. Stafford's NNC Company and Vause's troop of Native Horse who, dismounted, seem to have filled in to Mostyn's left and to the right of Younghusband's C Company, which had been sent out to cover the withdrawal from the plateau. The troops of Raw and Roberts had also withdrawn to the vicinity of Cavaye's company and similarly dismounted to join the firing line. Roberts himself had been killed during the withdrawal, possibly by a shot from Stuart Smith's artillery. At this stage, the Zulu were some 800 yards away, Stafford recalling that he adjusted the sights of one of his men to this range.

The possibility that the Zulu could approach in largely dead ground appears to have persuaded Pulleine to advance well forward of the camp, the two guns being stationed on a rocky knoll about 600 yards out from the nearest tent lines, with Porteous' A Company and Wardell's H Company to left and right respectively along a slight rocky ridge running roughly north-west to south-east. James Lonsdale's NNC Company – isiGquoza – had been on picket duty on the Nqutu plateau and out towards the Conical Kopje on the previous day. They appear to have been posted about half-way back to the camp from the Conical Kopje on the morning of the battle. They were then pulled back further at about the time when Durnford arrived in the camp and may or may not have filled in to the right of Wardell, this supposition arising from a map submitted by Essex to the subsequent Court of Inquiry, which Essex himself indicated might not have been accurate. It is also possible that Erskine's NNC Company – if not those men seen by Essex with Cavaye and Mostyn – were also posted to the left or right of Wardell, but there is no reliable information as to the exact positions occupied by the NNC in the firing line. Indeed, as F. W. D. Jackson has stated, there 'is no evidence whatsoever that the two wings of the 1/24th were separated by a body of native infantry' though there may have been some NNC between Younghusband and the companies of Cavaye and Mostyn.

Essentially, therefore, if any of the regulars were separated from the remainder by the NNC, it was Pope's company of the 2/24th off to the extreme right. Captain Krohn's NNC Company – probably amaBhele – was certainly held in reserve in front of the tents. According to his own account, Hamilton-Browne had sent back two NNC companies under the command of Captain Orlando Murray of the 2/3rd NNC to the camp with captured cattle some time on 21 January. There is no evidence at all as to their whereabouts during the battle though Murray was certainly among those killed at Isandlwana. It is possible, therefore, that Murray had returned to the camp without his men and that the subsequent disbandment of the 3rd NNC after Isandlwana may have led to some confusion on Hamilton-Browne's part. Some of Rupert Lonsdale's other officers and NCOs had returned to the camp without their men late on 21 January after apparently refusing to spend the night out in such an exposed position.

According to Glyn's interpreter, James Brickhill, Pulleine had received Chelmsford's message to strike camp and follow him at about 1200. Gardner did not state precisely what time he delivered the message but did mention in his evidence that it was about the time George Shepstone reported to Pulleine that his men were falling back before the Zulu on the plateau. Shepstone was directed to Pulleine's whereabouts by Brickhill. Shepstone stated bluntly, 'I'm not an alarmist, sir, but the Zulus are in such black masses over there, such long black lines that you have to give us all the assistance you can. They are now fast driving our men this way.' Gardner equally advised caution: 'Under the circumstances I should advise you disobeying the General's order, for the present at any rate. The General knows nothing of this, he is only thinking of the cowardly way in which the Zulus are running before our troops over yonder.' Therefore Pulleine, deciding that it was not possible to comply with Chelmsford's order for the time being, sent off another note to this effect: 'Heavy firing to the left of camp. Cannot move camp at present.' Gardner chose to amplify this further with his own message: 'Heavy firing near left of camp. Shepstone has come in for reinforcements, and reports the Zulus are falling back. The whole force at camp turned out and fighting about one mile to left flank.' Like Pulleine's first message to Chelmsford, these conveyed no real sense of danger, particularly Gardner's mistaken emphasis on a Zulu withdrawal, though, as it happened, and as already related, these messages did not reach Chelmsford until about 1500.

Another survivor who, like Brickhill, gave his testimony to Colonel Edward Bray at Umzinga, reported that the camp was being struck at the time when the battle was beginning out on the firing line. As suggested earlier, oxen had been yoked to some of the wagons before the attack began and other wagons were inspanned. Generally, the oxen, of course, had also been drawn in towards the camp earlier. It was later believed at the War Office that this was a prelude to a belated attempt at laagering, but it seems equally, if not more, likely that this was part of the process of moving camp, a point that will be raised again later.

Under the direction of Major Stuart Smith, who arrived back in camp with Gardner at just about the time that the deployment was ordered, the guns opened at once but the effective range of shrapnel was only some 1,200 yards and the opening range was about 3,400 yards. Moreover, the 7-pounder had a low muzzle velocity, which made it unsuitable for shrapnel. In all, Smith fired about 25 rounds of one kind or another. They do not appear to have done much damage to the Zulu – possibly because they may have remained unlimbered though Curling's letters suggest otherwise – and by the time the range was suitable for case shot, the British line was already withdrawing. For reasons seemingly dating from the earliest contacts between the Zulu and Europeans, the guns were called 'bye and bye' by the Zulu, a naval lieutenant in 1836 having reportedly answered Zulu inquiries as to the purpose of the guns by replying, 'You shall see bye and bye.'

According to Luke Sofikasho Zungu of the iNgobamakhosi, who recalled the battle in the 1930s, at least initially the 'bye and bye' compelled the Zulu to 'lie down like grass in a strong wind'. Other Zulu accounts, however, suggest that to minimise the impact the Zulu deliberately threw themselves down when they saw the gunners stand away from the guns at the moment of firing. Wally Erskine

Below: an imaginative view of the Zulu advance at Isandlwana. In fact, the warriors did not wear such finery in action.

of Stafford's company – not to be confused with Edward Erskine – remembered some Zulu shouting '*Qoka amatshe*' ('Catch stones') as the guns fired, an allusion to the boast of the umCijo that they would treat British bullets as stones. Others shouted '*uMoya*' ('Only wind'). At about 1215, Smith took one gun off more to the right to try and give supporting fire to Durnford. By this time, Durnford had fallen back to the Nyogane donga on the extreme right, which as previously indicated was about a mile in front of the camp. Pope's G Company of the 2/24th was extended to cover Durnford's rear though it was still at least 800 yards away from Durnford's position. At their farthest extent, the companies of Porteous and Wardell were at least half a mile forward of the camp. According to the written

report to the Inquiry by Curling, the two companies of the 1/24th also moved a further 30 yards beyond the guns when the Zulu had closed to about 400 yards, having advanced steadily in skirmishing order. Smith-Dorrien later said that the Zulu 'were in the most perfect order, and seemed to be in about 20 rows of skirmishers one behind the other' though it would appear that this was true more of the chest and left horn than the right horn.

This distance of 400 yards was usually regarded as the most effective range of the Martini-Henry. At this stage, therefore, as Smith-Dorrien later wrote in his memoirs, the 24th were more than holding their own: 'Possessed of splendid discipline and sure of success, they lay on their positions making every round tell, so much so that when the Zulu Army was 400 yards off it wavered.' Essex, too, remembered the men 'laughing, chattering and even joking as they unleashed volley after volley into the dense black masses'. In a letter published by *The Times* in April 1879, Essex also described the men as 'cheery as possible, making remarks to one another about their shooting'. To Essex it seemed the men 'thought they were giving the Zulus an awful hammering'. At this stage, the Zulu were described as humming like angry bees as they were kept at bay. One warrior, uMhoti of the umCijo, later recalled that 'we crouched down and dared not advance'. Some Zulu were using firearms and a number of men in the firing line were hit, including Stuart Smith, but, generally, the Zulu fire was too high. In large measure, the Zulu attack had stalled across the front of the camp. At some point between 1300 and 1330, however, the British line disintegrated.

5
TURNING-POINT
THE AMMUNITION CONTROVERSY

The exhaustion of ammunition in the firing line is one of the traditional explanations for this collapse, and still one of the most controversial. It was alleged that – among other failings – the ammunition boxes could not be unscrewed sufficiently quickly. In fact, the Mark V box used at Isandlwana had only one screw securing the wedge-shaped wooden panel that formed the lid of each stout box, after which it could be slid off without even removing the copper bands around the ends. Moreover, a sharp kick or blow from a rifle butt on the edge of the lid could open the boxes without recourse to the special screwdriver issued to quartermasters. The tin lining of the box was then drawn back by its attached handle.

Nor is there any real contemporary evidence that the supply failed. Only Essex mentioned ammunition to the Inquiry and he did so in the context of having organised various casuals to take out ammunition in a cart to Cavaye and Mostyn, who had been in action longest. Each man carried 70 rounds and it seems unlikely in the extreme that the additional 30 rounds per man specified by regulations if an engagement seemed likely were not issued in the period between 0800 and 1200. Admittedly, the ammunition carts of the 1/24th containing the 200 rounds kept in reserve for each man, were about a mile away from Cavaye and Mostyn. Overall, however, there were some 400,000 rounds in the camp since it included all the Column's reserve supplies.

Most officers favoured a steady and controlled rate of fire to ensure that it was effective. It was a matter of debate, however, whether independent or volley fire was the best means of achieving this. Major-General Henry Crealock, the brother of Chelmsford's military secretary, who was sent to Zululand with reinforcements in February 1879, declared himself in favour of volley firing in July. He argued that independent fire wasted ammunition and, in any case, men could not see through the smoke. Consequently, Crealock believed well-directed controlled volleys were the answer though evidence from other colonial campaigns suggests that volley firing was only 15 per cent effective even at the closest ranges. Based upon field firing tests, the manuals suggested that an independent rate of fire was almost twice as rapid as volley firing at either long or close range. It should also be noted, however, that even aimed fire was not necessarily likely to guarantee a large number of kills, and Zulu casualties were not as great as the British had anticipated. Indeed, it has been argued persuasively by Ian Knight that, on average, it may have taken 30–40 shots to kill one Zulu during the war as a whole, by no means an unusual ratio.

At Ulundi in July 1879, according to the war correspondent, Melton Prior, Chelmsford urged his troops, assembled in a square formation, 'Men, fire faster; can't you fire faster?' Prior pointedly contrasted this with Wolseley's advice to his men in Ashanti in 1873–74 to 'Fire slow, fire slow'. At Isandlwana, it is clear from the evidence of Smith-Dorrien and Essex that Wolseley's advice was initially followed. There was supervised independent fire at least by the companies of Cavaye, Mostyn and Younghusband, leading to the supposition that the rate of ammunition expenditure was not excessive. Volley firing is recorded only later in the action when the Zulu came within 400 yards, though it is conceivable that Wardell, Porteous and Pope adopted it as soon as they went into action. The duration of the main firefight was approximately 90 minutes at most. It should be noted that in other hotly contested actions during the war the expenditure of ammunition was low – an average of just 33 rounds per man over four hours at Khambula and just ten rounds in half an hour at Ulundi. In two hotly contested actions in the First Boer War of 1880–81, average expenditure of small arms ammunition was just over seventeen rounds at Laing's Nek (28 January 1881) and just over nineteen rounds at Ingogo (8 February 1881).

Glyn's groom, Private Williams, who survived, indicated that he had fired off his initial 70 rounds within an hour, but he was operating independently of supervision with other camp casuals, including Glyn's cook and three of Chelmsford's batmen. Williams fired 40–50 rounds 'when the Native Contingent fell back on the camp and one of their officers pointed out to me the enemy were

Below: British mounted infantry, c.1881, but not specifically of the Zulu War period, showing the mechanism of the Martini-Henry firearm. The man at the left is operating the lever-cum-trigger-guard to eject the cartridge of a fired round, while the man at the right has his trigger-guard down and thus the breech open, as he draws a cartridge from his pouch. An engraving by W. H. Dverend.

entering the right of the camp'. The remaining rounds (20–30) were fired when Williams and others 'went to the right'. Interestingly, Williams reports that Coghill then gave him orders to pack Glyn's tents on a wagon and to take Glyn's horses to the rear of the camp. Williams obtained another 40 rounds, using 29 of them before he left the camp shortly after Coghill, who told him to 'come on or I should get killed'. All the evidence suggests the men of the 24th were still firing repeatedly at the moment they fell back on the camp. As F. W. D. Jackson has stated: 'There is no reliable contemporary evidence that the regulars ran out of ammunition while in the line.'

The best-known testimony is that of the young Smith-Dorrien, who had not started back to the camp from Rorke's Drift until an hour after Durnford's departure from the post. But Smith-Dorrien made no statement on the issue of ammunition to the Inquiry. In a contemporary letter to his father, he simply said that he was out with the forward companies 'handing them spare ammunition'. In his much later memoirs, however, his account has him setting the casuals to work breaking open the ammunition boxes 'as fast as we could' and sending out packets to the firing line. More significantly, he implies that he was prevented from handing out ammunition to the native troops by Quartermaster Edward Bloomfield of the 2/24th. According to Smith-Dorrien, Bloomfield exclaimed, 'For heaven's sake don't take that, man, for it belongs to our battalion', to which Smith-Dorrien replied, 'Hang it man, you don't want a requisition now do you.'

In fact, it is clear that Bloomfield was killed at an early stage and, consequently, the conversation between Bloomfield and Smith-Dorrien may not have been decisive or meaningful. Smith-Dorrien may even have confused Bloomfield with James Pullen, the quartermaster of the 1/24th since it was Bloomfield who assisted Essex send out ammunition to Mostyn and Cavaye. Essex was also close to Bloomfield when he was shot. Cavaye and Mostyn were, it should be noted, in a different battalion from Bloomfield's. It might be added that Smith-Dorrien also recounted the story because, in his view, it spoke 'for the coolness and discipline of the regiment', presumably in admiration of Bloomfield's coolness under stress. It has also been suggested that the exchange between Smith-Dorrien and Bloomfield may have centred on the ammunition previously loaded for onward transmission to Chelmsford.

Pullen is variously described as trying to rally a group of men or preparing to flee, but, either way, this was clearly when the line had already collapsed. Hallam-Parr also suggested in his memoir of the war, published in 1880, that Mostyn and Cavaye ran low, but then he was with Chelmsford and not at Isandlwana. Moreover, the account of Private Bickley, one of the survivors of the 1/24th, a bandsman who was acting as picket sentry outside the officers' mess tent, suggests that fellow bandsmen, wagon drivers and other casuals were organised to carry ammunition out to the firing line. Despite the considerable degradation of the site by souvenir hunters over the years, recent archaeological investigations at Isandlwana have discovered a number of handles from the lining of the ammunition boxes out on the firing line. It has also turned up bent retaining screws suggestive of boxes broken open with rifle butts. Clearly, therefore, ammunition was reaching the firing line.

It is entirely feasible, of course, that the NNC, few of whom were armed with rifles anyway, did find it difficult to replenish their ammunition. Indeed, Essex later recalled of the period up on the plateau with Cavaye that the NNC 'blazed away at an absurd rate'. According to Wally Erskine, Barton tried and failed to obtain ammunition for the NNC at one stage and Barton himself later told Norris Newman that his men had been refused ammunition as 'it would all be required by the infantry themselves', compelling them to find their own ammunition wagons. Lonsdale's Company did apparently run out of ammunition but obtained a new supply, one survivor called Malindi testifying 'our ammunition failed once but we got fresh from the camp, and remained firing until the Zulus were within 100 yards'. Certainly, Durnford, whose men carried only 50 rounds for their Martini-Henry carbines, did run low, having held the position in the Nyogane donga for some 15 to 20 minutes. Henderson went back for ammunition at one stage and so did Davies with some of the Edendale men. According to Jabez Molife, they did reach their own ammunition wagons but at that very moment Durnford was forced back further towards the camp at about 1315. The probable location of Durnford's wagons well south of the track and well to the rear of the tents may suggest why so many of the Edendale and Hlubi men escaped, Molife implying that those sent back for the ammunition were cut off from the rest of the camp by the Zulu advance into it. Harry Davies, who escaped across Fugitives' Drift, certainly suggested later that Henderson 'escaped by the road' to Rorke's Drift though other evidence suggests that Henderson and the survivors of the Natal Native Horse crossed the river at or near Fugitives' Drift.

Difficulties could be experienced with the Martini's falling block lever action, which extracted the spent Boxer rolled brass cartridge, once the weapon became hot. The chamber itself became hot and affected by the greasy deposit left by the charge, the relatively thin cartridges then sticking in the chamber. If the extractor used then tore the cartridge, the remains had to be removed with a knife or similar instrument. When carried in either ammunition pouches or bullet bags for prolonged periods, cartridges could also become deformed. It might be added that it was by no means unusual for cartridges to be lost from the ball bags. As already related, Durnford cleared the mechanism for a number of his men, and one of the survivors of the Rocket Battery also testified that members of Nourse's company were having similar difficulties in extracting cartridges. It is significant that these examples relate to the NNH and NNC rather than the regulars, who would have been more accustomed to rectifying the problem. It is unlikely, therefore, that such problems contributed materially to the collapse of the British line.

Overheated barrels caused discomfort to the firer, and the more experienced troops sewed cowhide around the barrel to maintain their grip, but there was no ready remedy for the powerful recoil, which bruised shoulders. Moreover, the black powder charge of the cartridge produced a large amount of smoke, which could make visibility difficult in the event of rapid or prolonged fire. One survivor, George Mossop, recalled being 'almost choked' by the smoke and that he and others 'simply fired blind into it' with the result that none could 'concern himself with what was taking place elsewhere'. At Isandlwana, however, the firing line was so extended that smoke was probably not a major factor initially, though smoke and dust kicked up by men and animals subsequently might have inhibited the final defensive effort. Visibility was also partly affected by a partial eclipse of the sun commencing at about 1310, and reaching its height at 1429, by which time the British collapse was an accomplished fact. In retrospect the partial eclipse was probably more significant for the impact it made upon the Zulu participants. One Zulu from the uNokhenke, who spoke to Bertram Mitford when he visited Isandlwana in 1880, recalled that 'the sun turned black in the middle of the battle; we could still see it over us, or should have thought we had been fighting till evening'. Indeed, it is significant that the eclipse – at its peak obscuring about 65 per cent of the sun – is only mentioned in Zulu accounts and by none of the British survivors.

Durnford's retirement, which may well have triggered the collapse, may have been due to ammunition failure. One survivor, however, indicated that they were still firing from the saddle as they fell back and other accounts mention the Natal Native Horse firing volleys at the Zulu from the Natal bank at Fugitives' Drift. Indeed, it is more likely that Durnford retired because he felt that his position was now being dangerously outflanked by the uMbonambi: Durnford implied as much when briefly meeting Gardner after the retirement back on the camp. The uMbonambi also appear to have driven a small herd of cattle before them to disrupt Durnford's defence, using the cattle as cover for their advance. Once the line collapsed, however, so would have the organisation of the ammunition supply to the regulars, which would explain Zulu accounts of small groups of the 24th dying in hand-to-hand fighting in the camp once their ammunition was expended. Glyn's groom, Williams, claimed that ammunition was not reaching the line because 'I saw horses and mules with ammunition on their backs galloping about the camp', but it would appear that this was at a very late stage.

6

THE FALL OF THE CAMP

If failure of the ammunition supply was not the decisive factor, what then did cause the collapse of the British line?

In terms of the effect of Durnford's retreat, Gardner had taken the mounted volunteers out about a quarter of a mile; they were variously armed with Swinburne-Henry and Westley-Richards 'monkey-tail' carbines. He left them there under Captain Bradstreet to hold position, possibly in the Mpofane donga, in support of Durnford. It is possible that they may have joined him farther forward in the Nyogane. Durnford also appears to have come into the camp at one stage to gather some more reinforcements and conceivably to confer with Pulleine. Shortly afterwards, Gardner observed Bradstreet falling back. On riding forward to ascertain why, he discovered that Durnford had ordered them

Left: British infantry. Note the cased Colours behind the mounted officer in the background. A contemporary engraving.

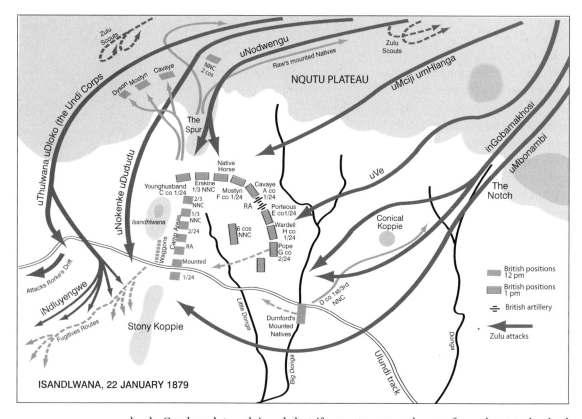

ISANDLWANA, 22 JANUARY 1879

back. Gardner later claimed that if even two squadrons of regular cavalry had been available, the entire Zulu advance could have been halted, but this seems unlikely. Durnford's retirement opened up the right flank, isolating Pope's Company which was in the process of extending further towards Durnford's position. In turn, Pope's extension to the right may have increased the Zulu pressure on whatever NNC men were positioned between Pope and Wardell.

Durnford's retirement may also have persuaded Pulleine to order a general withdrawal on the camp, particularly as many of the camp casuals were also apparently leaving in increasing numbers. Private E. Wilson of the 1/24th, a surviving bandsman who was acting as stretcher-bearer, recalled that when 'the idlers and men among the tents were now making the best of their way out of Camp, the doctor told us we were no longer likely to be of any use and the Band Sergeant told us we had better get away as best we could'. These casuals, of course, included many of those being utilised to take ammunition out to the firing line.

At the moment when the retirement was ordered – at least two survivors stated that bugles had sounded the retire – Porteous, Wardell and Stuart Smith's guns were, it will be recalled, at least half a mile in front of the camp and the Zulu were but 400 yards away from them. It is not perhaps surprising, therefore, that they were unable to beat the Zulu back to the camp. As uMhoti of the umCijo later testified: 'Then at the sound of a bugle, the firing ceased at a breath, and the whole British front rose from the ground and retired on the tents. Like a flame the whole Zulu force sprang to its feet and darted upon them.' Yet, since few British dead were found on the original perimeter, it is clear that the regulars fell back in relatively good order, though Uguku of the umCijo recalled: 'As we rushed on the soldiers retired on the camp, fighting all the way, and as they got into the camp we were intermingled with them …'

At this point, it is possible that the NNC broke. Gardner claimed that they did so at an early stage. Essex, by contrast, suggested that the NNC broke while he was talking with Durnford about the need to take some of the mounted men to prevent the Zulu from outflanking the camp still further. According to Essex it was this that uncovered the right and rear of the 1/24th companies on the left of the camp. While obviously unhelpful to the defence, this was not quite the same as the traditional image of a catastrophic collapse by the NNC in the centre of the line bringing about the disaster, especially as their precise whereabouts in the firing line cannot be determined accurately. In any case, it would seem that the collapse by Lonsdale's company and remaining elements of Barry's company followed as a consequence of the retirement rather than a trigger to it.

Wally Erskine had only just returned to Stafford's company on the left of the firing line, having gone back to the wagon line to find himself another gun – 'the one I had having got out of order in the breech' – when that company broke. His account is not entirely clear in terms of the sequence of events, but suggests that the flight of Stafford's men occurred before the retirement of both Durnford's force and those companies to the right of Smith's guns, since he then 'followed, firing as I went, thinking they were falling back on the camp'. It also suggests, however, that the Zulu were within 300 yards when the company fled. Krohn's company never came into action and broke as soon as the firing line retired. The official figures indicate that the heaviest NNC casualties occurred between the two companies of the 2/3rd NNC led by Barry and Erskine, each of which sustained at least 50 per cent losses. The dead included Pakhade's son, Gabangaye, though Sikhotha, who was also present at Isandlwana, survived.

Undoubtedly, a greater factor in the collapse was the extended nature of the British line. At full war establishment, a British infantry battalion consisted of 1,097 officers and men divided into eight companies. As suggested earlier with respect to the two battalions of the 24th, this was far from the reality. Companies were spread out with at least 200–300 yards between them, while each company in extended order also covered at least 200 yards in single file. In skirmishing order, there could be anything between four and ten paces between individual men. The conclusion of William Penn Symons of the 2/24th, who made a study of the battlefield, was that, on the right of the guns, the men were probably even farther apart. The firing line extended at least 2,000 yards from Younghusband to Pope.

Again, recent archaeological investigations have suggested that the firing line facing towards the iNyoni heights was farther forward from the camp (by some

200 yards) than is usually supposed, probably to make use of the dongas on the northern side of the camp and to deny the Zulu use of more dead ground. Crucially, it put the companies beyond Pulleine's direct sight. Pope's company may also have been initially deployed much farther out towards the Conical Kopje. Although Curling did not mention it to the Inquiry, his recently discovered letters also suggest that the actual number of men in the firing line was far fewer than is usually supposed. This was because the danger initially seemed slight and it was the intention to break camp. As Curling wrote: 'I suppose that not more than one half the men left in the camp took part in its defence as it was not considered necessary and they were left in as cooks etc.' Other evidence also suggests that the companies of the 24th were deployed with only an average of 50 men each in the firing line. This would imply only 300 or so in the firing line. In a telegram to his parents, Curling also indicated that, prior to Smith's return to the camp, he had himself taken out only 20 of the 74 artillerymen in the camp with the guns at 1100.

It has been plausibly suggested by Adrian Greaves and by Ron Lock and Peter Quantrill that the rest of the regulars were employed on packing up the camp since Pulleine probably wished to comply as far as possible with Chelmsford's orders. It has also been suggested, therefore, that this may explain why the tents were not struck in accordance with the regulations relating to an attack on the camp. Normally, packing the camp would have been a lengthy affair; more than 300 tents were required to accommodate the European troops alone, the NNC making do with makeshift shelters. Thus, striking the tents hurriedly by kicking

Below: Looking out towards the Conical Kopje and the iNyoni heights, the dongas that cross the plain in front of the camp and the broken nature of the terrain can be clearly discerned. (I. Beckett)

down the poles would have required re-erecting them before they could be properly packed. Had Pulleine ordered the tents to be struck and the Zulu threat not then materialised, he would have incurred criticism from Chelmsford for the delay in packing up the camp as well as appearing an alarmist.

There were also at least 80 men of the 2/24th not attached to G Company still in the camp for various reasons, many of them from A Company. It is possible that they were formed into a composite company under the two officers of the 2/24th who had returned to the camp with Gardner. The evidence, however, rests on a particular interpretation of a chance remark by Higginson that he passed five companies of the 24th marching out with the guns. Thus, when Wally Erskine went back to the wagon line for a second rifle, George Shepstone was urging 'soldiers and others left in charge of the baggage' to go out to the firing line as every man was needed there.

As it happened, Pulleine had deployed his men approximately in accordance with the instructions Chelmsford had issued to his column commanders in December 1878. British infantry and guns were forward, the NNC 'well clear of each flank' and 'well to the rear of each flank' of the regulars, and mounted infantry covering the flanks. Roughly the same deployment was used by Pearson in his action at Nyezane on the same day as Isandlwana. Consequently, the forward deployment was not some whim of an inexperienced Pulleine.

Another factor, of course, was the enemy for, as George Pickett once remarked when asked why his 'Charge' had failed at Gettysburg in July 1863, 'I think the Union Army had something to do with it.' The Zulu were most certainly not 'kaffirs, who

had only to be hunted' as Clery had suggested on one occasion. Chelmsford himself in a letter to Frere on 23 January remarked, 'The desperate bravery of the Zulu has been the subject of much astonishment', though he also suggested that the Zulu had succeeded principally 'by force of recklessness and numbers'. After the initial disorganisation, the Zulu quickly recovered and moved steadily on towards the British line. When the Zulu attack was stalled, for example, senior *izidunas* urged the umCijo to advance, including Mkhosana kaMundlane and Ndlaka, the latter crying, 'The little branch of leaves that beats out the fire [Cetshwayo] did not order this.' Ndlaka, who had been sent down from the plateau by the Zulu command, probably located on the outcrop of the plateau known as Mkwene, was shot dead almost at once, but the umCijo charged with renewed vigour. Equally, Sikizane kaNomageje, an *induna* of the iNgobamakhosi, called on his men not to allow the umCijo the honour of getting into the camp first. Subsequently, the Zulu decided that the honour of being first among the tents belonged to the uMbonambi, then the iNgobamakhosi and only then the umCijo. According to an anonymous Zulu deserter, it was the umCijo that had suffered most from both artillery and rifle fire and the uNokhenke from rifle fire.

The Zulu had never before faced such firepower as they confronted at Isandlwana and it says much for their courage and tenacity that they not only endured it, but also overcame it to push home their attack. This was particularly so given that those regiments in the forefront of the attack were the youngest and least experienced.

It has been suggested in a recent Channel Four documentary in the 'Secrets of the Dead' series that the Zulu battle preparations included the use of stimulants; the snuff used by the Zulu containing a particularly potent form of ground cannabis. Coupled with the normal pre-battle psychological stimulus, such a powerful drug could have enhanced fighting performance. Some Zulu were also likely to be determined to prove equal to the honoured status of *abaqawe* (heroes) by displaying reckless courage. The suddenness with which the action had begun, however, meant that the customary rituals were swiftly truncated at Isandlwana. If anything, therefore, such an explanation for Zulu prowess actually detracts from their achievement.

Indeed, it seems difficult to refute the argument advanced by Reginald Coupland back in 1948 that, even if Chelmsford had not managed to divide his force on 22 January, a Zulu attack on the following day would have been just as successful. Chelmsford 'would have dined and gone to bed in his headquarters with the same sense of security as on the two previous nights'. Rather similarly, it seems equally unlikely that Chelmsford could either have saved his camp if he had returned to it on receipt of Pulleine's first message, or avoided an even more comprehensive defeat *en route* to it if caught in the open by the Zulu.

LAST STAND AND THE FUGITIVES' TRAIL

7

After Pulleine, or possibly Durnford, ordered the withdrawal, most men appear to have got back into the camp. The bodies of the 24th were found later largely in groups in the area of the 1/24th's tents to the south of the camp line, which suggests that the outlying companies in the north and centre had withdrawn right through the camp. Only the body of Colour-Sergeant Woolfe of Wardell's company and some 20 others in one group were found out close to the original firing line. About 70 bodies were found among the officers' tents of the 1/24th

Below: An imaginative view of the Zulu attacking the British line at Isandlwana by the artist, Richard Caton Woodville. The British line is backed (erroneously) by unfurled Colours as well as by mounted officers. (I. Beckett)

with another 60, including those of Wardell and Lieutenant Dyer of the 2/24th, close by but lower down in the camp area. At least one group forced back over the nek stood shoulder to shoulder or in a square formation when their ammunition ran out, but were broken up by the Zulu throwing spears at them rather than getting within range of the men's bayonets.

The one company seemingly cut off from the camp was that of Younghusband, which retreated up the slope of Isandlwana itself. There are various Zulu accounts of the remnant of Younghusband's company – about 70 bodies were later found together including those of Younghusband and his subaltern, Lieutenant George Hodson – eventually charging down. According to a Zulu of the uNokhenke interviewed by Bertram Mitford in 1882, 'There was an *induna* in front of them with a long flashing sword, which he whirled round his head as he ran – it must have been made of fire. Wheugh! (Here the narrator made an expressive gesture of shading his eyes.) They killed themselves by running down, for our people got above them and quite surrounded them; these, and a group of white men on the nek, were the last to fall.' One man – possibly an officer – held off the Zulu from a wagon bed for some time until he was shot. One of Younghusband's men was almost certainly the last to die, occupying a cave high up on the mountain until shot at about 1700. Less well known than Fripp's painting, Richard Moynan's 'The Last of the 24th', painted in 1884, depicted this particular episode. According to Mangwanana Mcunu of the uVe, whose account was written down in the 1930s, another soldier chased up to the top of Isandlwana could speak Zulu and appealed to one of his pursuers, 'Do not kill me in the sun, kill me in the shadows', before being stabbed. A few soldiers also appear to have either fallen or been thrown from the top of the mountain.

Durnford died with about 60 or so men on the saddle and slopes of Black's Kopje, having apparently told the Hlubi and Edendale men to leave, Simeon Kambule keeping the latter together. Durnford's brother later claimed that his watch had stopped at 1520, but this was probably some time after his actual death. It was noted later that his body was surrounded by that of Natal Carbineers, who had been most critical of him after their experience at Bushman's Pass six years earlier, and other colonial volunteers. Zulu accounts also recall the distinctive figure of Durnford – tall, moustached and with his useless left arm in a sling – inspiring this small group in its attempt to hold back the Zulu left horn.

The monument of the Natal Carbineers recalls in its epitaph the famous last stand in antiquity at Thermopylae. Sihayo's son, Mehlokazulu, remembered the stand of the Carbineers: 'They threw down their guns when their ammunition was done, and they commenced with their pistols, which they used as long as their ammunition lasted; and then they formed a line, shoulder to shoulder, and back to back, and fought with their knives.' Another Zulu, Kumbeka Gwabe of the umCijo recalled in 1929 that he had managed to kill only one man: 'Dum! Dum! went his revolver as he was firing from right to left, and I came along beside him and stuck my assegai under his right arm, pushing it through his body until it came out between his ribs on the left side. As soon as he fell I pulled the assegai out and slit his stomach so that I knew that he would not shoot any more of my people.'

There are varying accounts of Pulleine's death, one being that he was killed in his tent while writing a last letter. Another version has Pulleine with 40 or so men dying just to the rear of the saddle though his body appears to have been found in the 1/24th camp area. As will be indicated later, Coghill already knew that Pulleine had been killed when he met Curling and Melvill during the retreat. One later Zulu account told of two officers killed together. One was shot but the other fired his revolver at the warrior, grazing his neck and wounding his leg. The Zulu threw his assegai, which struck the officer in the chest. Staggering back, the officer tried to pull it out, at which point in his account the Zulu 'writhed his body in pantomime of the movements of the officer'. The Zulu killed him with another assegai. As the Zulu said the two both had 'pieces of glass' in their eyes, they are usually taken to be Pope and his fellow subaltern of the 2/24th, Lieutenant Frederick Godwin-Austen, both of whom habitually wore a monocle.

Below: C. E. Fripp's celebrated painting of the last stand of the 24th at Isandlwana first exhibited in 1885. Fripp's depiction of the landscape is very accurate. (National Army Museum)

George Shepstone took some of the NNC – possibly from either Erskine's or Murray's companies – to the rear of Isandlwana, trying to hold open the line of retreat from the Zulu right horn; his body was found with perhaps 100 others on the south-western slope of the mountain. Many bodies of the 24th were found behind the nek in dongas to the right of the road, that of Anstey and a group of

about 60 men of the 24th being found on the banks of the Manzimyama stream some two miles behind the mountain.

The Zulu, uMhoti, recalled struggling with one soldier whom he first stabbed in the shoulder: 'He dropped his rifle and seized me round the neck, and threw me on the ground under him, my eyes felt as if they were bursting and I almost

Left: 'At Bay: The Battle of Isandula' [sic: contemporary spelling of Isandlwana]. An engraving by Durand.

Below: Surgeon-Major
Peter Shepherd, killed
as he stopped to tend
a wounded man at
the beginning of the
retreat from the camp,
was commemorated
by the St. John
Ambulance
Association, with
which he had close
connections, by the
issue of his aide-
memoire on first aid.
(I. Beckett)

choked when I succeeded in grasping the spear which was still sticking in his shoulder and forced it into his vitals and he rolled over, lifeless.' According to the Zulu, Nzuzi, some of the British who spoke Zulu called for mercy. Others, said Muziwento 'covered their faces with their hands, not wishing to see death. Some ran away. Some entered into the tents. Others were indignant; although badly wounded they died where they stood, at their post.'

There are brief glimpses of others in the last moments as the defence disintegrated: Milne's sailor servant, Able Seaman Aynsley, was seen with his back to a wagon, defending himself with his cutlass. Lieutenant Daly of F Company of the 1/24th waved to the mounted men as they left the camp. Stafford heard another officer shout, '24th, Fix bayonets!' Kambule tried unsuccessfully to persuade a young drummer boy, who insisted that he had been told to stay by an officer, to leave an ammunition wagon. James Pullen rallied a small group near the Stony Kopje with the words, 'Come on, men rally here, follow me. Don't be running away like a parcel of women. Let's try and turn their flank.' Trooper H. T. Pearce of the Natal Mounted Police turned back to retrieve his horse's bit from his tent though urged to leave by his friend, Trooper Charles Sparks. Some refused to run away. Preparing to flee with Raw, the Hon. Standish William Vereker of Barry's NNC Company, the son of Viscount Gort, gave up a horse claimed by an African auxiliary. James Lonsdale gave his horse to Malindi and turned to join one of the groups of regulars. One account has Surgeon Major Peter Shepherd killed when stopping to assist a wounded man.

The desperate struggle in and around the nek kept the Zulu horns from closing sufficiently and enabled some to flee, the Zulu pursuit of the fugitives in itself probably contributing to the opening of a temporary gap. The survivors, including some who had undoubtedly decided at an early stage that discretion was the better part of valour, were forced over the saddle and down towards the Buffalo, about

First Aid to the Injured.

St. John Ambulance Association.

- -

A POCKET

AIDE-MEMOIRE

COMPILED

FOR THE INSTRUCTION OF THE TROOPS IN ZULULAND,

BY THE LATE

SURGEON-MAJOR P. SHEPHERD, M.B.,

SHORTLY BEFORE HIS DEATH

At Isandula, January 22, 1879.

- -

Reprinted for the use of St. J.A.A. pupils.

Copies can be obtained from the Honorary Director

of Stores, St. John's Gate, Clerkenwell, London, E.C.

Price 3d. each. By post, 4d.,

Or in Packets of One Dozen, 3s.

three and half miles away. What became known as the Fugitives' Trail was a nightmare of gullies and broken ground. The survivors had to negotiate first a stony stream bed, followed by a deep donga, then the steep banks of the Manzimyama stream, then the Mpethe ridge, and then the descent to the Buffalo itself at Sothondose's Drift, soon to be renamed Fugitives' Drift. The river was in full spate and included both a whirlpool and a rocky gorge, through which the water took on the characteristics of a torrent. So bad was the ground for the horses that the Zulu were easily able to keep up with those fleeing on horseback. The artillery had galloped through the camp, but one gun overturned and the other was caught in a ravine about 400 yards beyond the nek. There had been no time to spike either gun and they were both later hauled away by the Zulu, both being discovered dismounted from their carriages in a donga close to Ulundi by a cavalry patrol in August 1879.

The gunners were nearly all killed while running through the camp behind the guns, Curling having thought that they would be able to take up a position further back, but the Zulu were already behind them. Only twelve members of the Royal Artillery survived from the 74 in the camp. Other men had clung to the guns and limbers, but were then caught and killed also. Stuart Smith was stabbed through the arm and was subsequently killed beside Smith-Dorrien, the latter having stopped temporarily to tend to a wounded man from the mounted infantry. His horse having bolted, Smith-Dorrien, according to his contemporary letter to his father, 'with the strong hope that everybody clings to that some accident would turn up ... rushed off on foot and plunged into the river ...' On the Natal bank, having lost his horse in the river but having got across by grabbing another's tail, he lay on his back to drain the water out of his boots and then caught another horse. He offered a ride to Conductor James Hamer of the Commissariat Department, only for Hamer to promptly ride off without him, forcing him to continue on foot.

Stafford of the NNC described the flight as 'perfect pandemonium' while Brickhill wrote that 'our stampede was composed of mules, oxen, horses and flying men – all strongly intermingled, man and beast apparently all infected with the danger which surrounded us ...' Brickhill, who had refused to stop to help Band-Sergeant David Gamble of the 1/24th, also noted that the trail was 'strewn with shields, assegais, blankets, hats, clothing of all description, guns, ammunition belts, saddles (which horses had managed to kick off), revolver and belt and I don't know what not'. Essex remembered 'an awful ride of ten miles, and I cannot describe the terrible scenes I witnessed further than to say that the Zulus take no prisoners, but employ the assegai in every case'. Cochrane reached the river 'with a good horse, hard riding, and good luck'.

Others had equally miraculous escapes. Harry Davies wrote of a Zulu catching hold of his bridle. Davies tried to stab him with his carbine's bayonet, 'but the man caught hold of it and pulled it out of my hand, which at the same time made my horse rear and cleared me of the man. I then had only my revolver, and I saw a Zulu right in my course, and rode at him and shot him in the neck. My horse got a stab, and many assegais were thrown at me; but, as I was lying along my horse, they did not hit me.' Wally Erskine was hit in the leg by an assegai thrown by one Zulu and, having been fired at by another, demanded in Zulu, 'Who the hell do you think you're firing at?' Astonished, the Zulu let Erskine pass. If they reached the river, many of the survivors including Erskine owed their lives to covering fire from the Edendale Troop and some of Sikali's Horse, who had been rallied on the Natal bank by Barton and Raw with the assistance of Kambule.

Curling caught up with Coghill twice, Coghill telling him on the first occasion that he did not think it would be possible to stage any rally, and on the second that Pulleine was dead. Near the river, Curling saw Melvill with the Queen's Colour of the 1/24th. Melvill, who may or may not have been ordered to save the Colour by Pulleine, managed to reach the river despite being encumbered by the staff and case, the Colour itself being some four feet by 3½ feet in size when unfurled. His horse, however, lost its feet in the river and Melvill was swept

Below: A view from the saddle looking down the beginning of Fugitives' Trail behind Isandlwana. The line of cairns marks the retreat of surviving groups of soldiers. (I. Beckett)

towards a prominent rock to which Walter Higginson was already clinging. In the process, Melvill lost his grip on the Colour and neither he nor Higginson could retrieve it. Having reached the river ahead of Melvill and almost certainly having left Isandlwana well before him, Coghill rode back in to try and assist him, but his horse was immediately shot. Reaching the Natal bank, Higginson ostensibly went to find horses, since he, too, had lost his mount in the torrent. According to the account of Penn Symons, presumably from Higginson's testimony, Coghill had said, 'I am done, I can go no further', and Melvill, 'Neither can I,' though it is entirely possible that Melvill deliberately stayed to help Coghill, who was hindered, of course, by his leg injury.

In the event, Higginson was given a horse by a Natal Carbineer, Trooper William Barker, and, like Hamer in the case of Smith-Dorrien, made off immediately though he claimed that he had realised that Melvill and Coghill had been overwhelmed. Fortunately for Barker, some of his comrades, who subsequently came across Higginson, rode back and rescued him. Meanwhile, Melvill and

Coghill struggled about half a mile up from the river, to be killed near the top of the heights on the Natal side. Melvill's watch was later found to have stopped at 1410, presumably when he was first thrown into the water.

Ironically, it is now believed that Zulu in pursuit did not kill Melvill and Coghill since few Zulu ventured to cross the swollen river. Three regiments of the uNdi corps, for example, crossed the Buffalo close to where it met the Batshe to attack Rorke's Drift by forming human chains. Moreover, the Zulu well knew that Cetshwayo had instructed them not to cross the river: Vumandaba kaNtati, an influential *induna* of the umCijo reputedly shouted to the iNgobamakhosi not to disobey the King when some started to cross at Fugitives' Drift though the King's own brother, Ndabuko, had unsuccessfully tried to get the uMbonambi to do so.

It is possible that those who killed Melvill and Coghill were members of the iNdluyengwe. It will be recalled that they had been committed to the pursuit and that they did ford the Buffalo farther up from Fugitives' Drift where the water was calmer, before making their way to join the remainder of the uNdi corps at Rorke's Drift. It is considered more likely, however, that the perpetrators were followers of Sihayo's brother, Gamdana kaXongo, who had pledged allegiance to the British. Some accounts suggest that Gamdana's people had been incensed, however, by the detention of eight of their number as spies by Chelmsford when they had appeared at the camp as a sign of Gamdana's goodwill. Chelmsford had released the men the day before the attack on the camp, hence the number of accounts claiming that it was the very men released who had killed Melvill and Coghill. Some accounts also have it that some of Gamdana's men came into the camp to surrender some rifles on 22 January and were interviewed by Durnford before he set out on his ride across the plain. Either way, not all Gamdana's followers, particularly the younger men, shared their chief's new found loyalty to the British. Alternatively, those who killed Melvill and Coghill may have been followers of Sothondose, Zulu long settled on the Natal bank, who had been watching events and had been urged to kill survivors by the pursuers calling across the river that they would face retribution if they did not do so.

A party led by Major Wilsone Black of the 2/24th discovered the bodies of Melvill and Coghill on 4 February. According to one account, the bodies were not alone, but with those of two dead soldiers of the mounted infantry. Harford found the Colour and case downstream on the following day. Subsequently, of course, the Queen herself placed a wreath of *immortelles* on the Colour's staff. The Regimental Colour of the 1/24th had been back at Helpmekaar. The Colours of the 2/24th had also been in the camp, but were never recovered. A part of one of the staffs was found on Stony Kopje and a part of another on the Fugitives' Trail, which might suggest a similar attempt to carry it to safety.

The principal report on the demise of Melvill and Coghill was written by Glyn, who appears to have consciously presented their story in the most heroic light possible in order to further help the process of retrieving something from the disaster. There was certainly no actual evidence on which Glyn could have concluded that Pulleine entrusted the Colour to Melvill with the words, 'You, as senior subaltern, will take the Colour and make your way from here.' The story, however, soon became a necessary myth. A poem by J. E. Carpenter, 'The Saving of the Colours' eulogising Melvill and Coghill appeared in *The Graphic* as early as 15 March alongside the first speculative engraving of the battle for the camp. Subsequently, Alphonse de Neuville, who had already painted a version of Rorke's Drift in 1880, produced two paintings in 1882 commemorating the two subalterns. 'Saving the Queen's Colour' depicted Melvill and Coghill leaving the camp, while 'The Last Sleep of the Brave' depicted the discovery of their corpses, the Colour draped across them. Fripp, whose well-known painting of Isandlwana has already been mentioned, had also done a large-scale watercolour, 'Dying to Save the Queen's Colours' in 1881.

Melvill and Coghill also soon became the focus of a campaign for the award of the Victoria Cross. Sir Garnet Wolseley, who superseded Chelmsford in May 1879, for one considered it undesirable to make heroes of men 'who taking advantage of their having horses bolted from the scene of action to save their lives'. Even Chelmsford questioned whether Melvill would have received the VC if he had saved the Colour and himself and, though he may well have been ordered to leave the camp: 'he no doubt was given the best chance of saving his life which must have been lost had he remained in camp'. Moreover, Chelmsford did not think that Coghill was capable through his injury of having participated in any attempt to save the Colour and must have been 'a drag on poor Melvill' so that Melvill had 'lost his life endeavouring to save Coghill rather than vice versa'. As it happened, the warrant for the VC did not allow for posthumous awards or, rather, assuming that it did not had become a matter of convention. Consequently, the army's Commander-in-Chief, the Duke of Cambridge, wrote to Melvill's father in April 1879 indicating that his son would have won the VC had he survived. Melvill's widow also received an annual pension of £100 at the request of the Queen. When more cases arose during the South African War (1899–1902), Coghill's father raised the matter again. The new King, Edward VII, twice refused to relent on the rule, but when Melvill's widow directly petitioned him in December 1906, he changed his mind. The rule was finally altered in January 1907, Melvill and Coghill being honoured together with four others, the gallantry of two of whom dated back to the Indian Mutiny.

The one VC that was awarded at the time for Isandlwana went to Private Samuel Wassall of the 80th, attached to the Mounted Infantry, for saving the life of Private Thomas Westwood, also detached from the 80th, at Fugitives' Drift. Wassall, who had already crossed the torrent returned at once to the Zulu bank when he saw Westwood in trouble. Wassall had the presence of mind to secure his pony to a tree before plunging back into the water to drag out Westwood, remounting with him and then crossing once more to the Natal bank and safety. As it happened, an existing holder of the VC was killed at Isandlwana, Private William Griffiths of the 2/24th having received the award for saving lives in a

storm off the Andaman Islands in May 1867. The rules were changed soon thereafter and Griffiths was only one of six men ever awarded the VC for gallantry not
performed in the face of the enemy, four of the others also being awarded for the
same incident off the Andamans.

It is usually suggested that a total of 445 individuals escaped from the field, but
this may over-estimate the number of African survivors, of whom only 85 are def-
initely known. While the traditional total for European survivors is 55, the actual

Right: Fugitives' Drift
viewed from the Natal
bank. The top of the
large black rock to
which Melvill and
Henderson clung can
be seen in the lower
centre of the photo-
graph. At the time, of
course, the river was
in full spate.
(I. Beckett)

total appears to be 78 known European survivors with a further two probable and fourteen whose fates are unknown. Certainly only five European survivors were regular officers – Smith-Dorrien, Curling, Essex, Gardner, and Cochrane. Curling rather uncharitably wrote to his mother that most European survivors were colonials or NNC officers and NCOs 'who tell any number of lies'. As it happened, all five surviving regulars were wearing blue patrol jackets, which may give credence to Cetshwayo's supposed instruction to kill all those in red coats.

Once on the Natal bank, Gardner conferred with Essex and Cochrane and sent a message to Rorke's Drift and another to Helpmekaar, going on to the latter himself. Reaching Helpmekaar, Gardner wanted to send a message to warn Evelyn Wood, but when none of the Basutos would take it, rode off himself to find Wood, finally sending the latter a message from Utrecht and then returning to Helpmekaar. Two privates from the Mounted Infantry squadron, Edward Evans of the 3rd Foot and Daniel Whelan of the 1/13th Foot, carried Gardner's message to Rorke's Drift. Evans, who lost his rifle crossing Fugitives' Drift when briefly unhorsed, later wrote that 'I could never explain half what I have seen, nor how I was saved.' In all, just ten members of the 24th escaped the field: four men attached to the Mounted Infantry, three survivors from Russell's rocket battery; the bandsmen, Bickley and Wilson; and Glyn's groom, Williams.

Below:
Sir Evelyn Wood.

Another of those who reached Rorke's Drift (at about 1515 or 1530) was the mysterious Lieutenant Adendorff of Krohn's Company of the 1/3rd NNC. Adendorff, who claimed to have escaped Isandlwana 'by the road' had met Lieutenant J. Vane of the NNC, who had escaped down the Fugitives' Trail. Other survivors continued to pass the post. Henderson arrived with a party of the Hlubi Troop at about 1530. At the request of Chard, who had now assumed command as senior officer – Major Spalding had left for Helpmekaar to speed along Captain Russell Upcher and Thomas Rainforth's companies of the 1/24th at about 1400 with the immortal words, 'Nothing will happen and I shall be back again this evening early' – Henderson threw out his men as advanced pickets. On the first appearance of the Zulu at about 1620, however, they rapidly fled. According to Bob Hall, a civilian cattle dealer attached to the Commissariat Department, but who also appears to have served in the Natal Mounted Police, he and Henderson fired a few shots before deciding to make for Helpmekaar. Subsequently Henderson and Hall met Spalding, who was returning to Rorke's Drift with D and G Companies of the 1/24th from Helpmekaar. When Spalding decided to retire on Helpmekaar, Henderson went with him while Hall went off after his cattle. Hall's account, however, dates from at least 27 years after the event, and the only known letters of Henderson make no mention of Rorke's Drift at all. The flight of the Natal Native Horse had an immediate knock-on effect upon Captain William Stephenson's abaThembu company of the 2/3rd NNC, one of whose fleeing white NCOs was shot down by the outraged defenders.

According to Chard's official report, Adendorff remained to assist in the defence, thus theoretically being the only man to fight at both Isandlwana and Rorke's Drift. Considerable doubt, however, has always surrounded Adendorff's role. It is now believed that Chard mistakenly attributed to Adendorff actions undertaken during the struggle for Rorke's Drift by Corporal Francis Attwood of the Army Service Corps. It is also believed that both Vane and Adendorff were subsequently arrested, but no further action was taken, possibly because any proceedings would have reflected adversely upon Chard's report and because Vane was apparently ordered to carry his warning to the garrison at Helpmekaar by Bromhead. As it happens, it has been argued recently and persuasively by Adrian Greaves that Chard was not the actual author of his report on the action at Rorke's Drift, the most likely candidate being Clery.

In the event, Chard and Bromhead with some 118 active defenders, famously saw off some 3–4,000 Zulu from the uThulwana, iNdluyengwe, uDloko and iNdlondo during the night of 22/23 January. Eleven VCs were awarded in an action which, of course, proved the effectiveness of even improvised fortifications when coupled with British firepower.

Interestingly, cases were also made for the VC to be awarded to Gardner, Higginson and Adendorff. Pointedly, Chelmsford rejected any consideration of Adendorff on the grounds that his early arrival at Rorke's Drift suggested that he had left Isandlwana 'way before he had any right to do so'. Higginson's failure to return to help Melvill and Coghill after he went off for horses seems to have ruled him out. In the case of Gardner, a campaign by some of his friends to have him awarded the VC proved counter-productive. Moreover, rumours began to circulate that his departure from Helpmekaar in search of Wood had been somewhat hasty, a little ditty going the rounds, 'I very much fear that the Zulus are near so hang it, I'm off to Dundee.' Certainly, another survivor, Dugald MacPhail of the Buffalo Border Guard, believed Gardner so unnerved by his experiences at Isandlwana and in the retreat to be 'off his head' with any noise making him 'suddenly start'. Isandlwana, of course, had been a traumatic experience for all. Mention has already been made of the effect upon those who returned to the camp with Chelmsford on the night of 22 January. Glyn, Russell, Harness and even Colonel Fairfax Hassard of the Royal Engineers, who only presided over the subsequent inquiry, all displayed symptoms of stress and Curling was also described, ironically by Harness, as 'a good deal shaken'.

8
AFTERMATH

Below: The return of Chelmsford's force to Isandlwana on the evening of 22 January 1879 as depicted by *The Graphic*. The figure **1** in the centre marks the location of the camp. (I. Beckett)

It was fortunate that Rorke's Drift could be manipulated to deflect attention from Isandlwana, much as the defeat of Wood at Hlobane in March 1879 was to be effectively cancelled out by his crushing victory over the Zulu at Khambula on the following day. It was also claimed that Rorke's Drift had saved Natal from a Zulu invasion though, of course, Cetshwayo had no intention of this. Rorke's Drift did not, however, prevent considerable panic in the border districts of Natal, with hasty laagers being formed for civilians at a number of locations such

as Ladysmith, Newcastle, Dundee (Fort Pine), Stanger, Greytown and Pietermaritzburg while plans were also made to fortify key buildings in Durban. Forts were hastily constructed at other locations including Helpmekaar, and on the Greytown to Helpmekaar road. As a precaution, what remained of the 3rd NNC was disbanded in its entirety and the 2nd NNC was dissolved temporarily.

Rorke's Drift, however, did not prevent rising criticism of Chelmsford and Frere. Having read Chelmsford's dispatch on the affair, for example, one of the officers of the 1/24th, Lieutenant William Lloyd, wrote: 'Ld. C better take care or he may find that certain things he did *not* mention in his drivelling report may come out.' Blame had to be attributed, therefore, because, as Richard Stevens of the Natal Mounted Police wrote after his escape, 'There will be an awful row at home about this.' Conveniently deceased, Durnford was an obvious scapegoat though, as suggested earlier, there was also some attempt to shift blame to Glyn.

Chelmsford's hastily convened Court of Inquiry on the disaster at Isandlwana held on 27 January simply officially recorded the statements of Clery, Glyn, Gardner, Essex, Cochrane, Smith-Dorrien, Curling and Nourse. Those of Glyn and Smith-Dorrien were so brief as to add nothing to the story, while Essex and Curling confined themselves to submitting written statements. Interestingly Curling later wrote that he had had no idea that the proceedings would be published and few of those called had therefore taken the trouble 'to make a readable statement'. The three members of the court – Hassard of the Royal Engineers, the next senior officer to Chelmsford in South Africa, and Lieutenant-Colonels Francis Law and Arthur Harness of the Royal Artillery – reached no conclusion because 'instructions on this point were not given to it'. It may even be that Harness was placed on the Inquiry to ensure that he could not give evidence himself. Responding to later criticism, Harness himself was careful to draw a distinction between the instructions to investigate 'the loss of the camp' and any investigation of the 'circumstances of the disastrous affair'. The former was strictly limited to ascertaining 'what orders were given for the defence of the camp, and how these orders were carried out'. In fact, a number of other statements were taken. But Harness, who seems to have taken a far more active role than Hassard or the generally indolent Law, decided which statements to include in the official account. Harness later stated that there was no point recording 'statements hardly bearing on the loss of the camp but giving doubtful particulars of

Below: Isandlwana photographed by a Natal-based photographer, James Lloyd, during the expedition back to the field to bury the dead in June 1879. (National Army Museum)

small incidents more or less ghastly in their nature'. Harness also wrote to his brother of other evidence either merely corroboratory of that already recorded or 'so unreliable that it was worthless', suggesting that if a 'mass of statements' was intended it could have been recorded by 'three subalterns or three clerks'.

In transmitting the findings, such as they were, to Chelmsford, however, Colonel William Bellairs, the DAG, deduced that the blame lay with Durnford for not obeying the orders directed to Pulleine. This became Chelmsford's principal argument in a speech to the House of Lords in August 1880. Frere took a similar view of Durnford's guilt, though, interestingly, an internal War Office memorandum in

February 1879 largely ascribed the blame to Chelmsford for not fortifying his camp, for not keeping in contact with the enemy, and for being 'decoyed' by the Zulu. The Duke of Cambridge did his best to defend Chelmsford, trying to make the latter comprehend the requirements of domestic public opinion and to provide a coherent account of his conduct sufficient to refute press criticism. Although deeply conservative, Cambridge was no fool and wanted answers, hence the attempt made by Chelmsford and Crealock, referred to earlier, to suggest that Glyn was in command of No 3 Column in all respects. Cambridge, however, ultimately concluded that Chelmsford had fatally underestimated the Zulu and, it would seem, had little doubt that the blame for the defeat lay firmly with Chelmsford.

Apart from Wilsone Black's brief foray to Fugitives' Drift in February, there was no further attempt to reach the battlefield until 14 March when a larger patrol under Black briefly visited the scene, but retired when they encountered some Zulu. Another patrol led by Black again visited the site on 15 May, at which time Lieutenant Pope's diary was recovered from the field with its last entry written mid morning on 22 January: 'Durnford Basutos, arrive and pursue. – Rocket Battery. Zulus retire everywhere. Men fall out for dinners.' Stuart Smith's body was also found on the Fugitives' Trail. Subsequently, on 21 May, a still larger group arrived under Major-General Frederick Marshall, the intention being not only to bury remains but also to recover wagons. Some 45 vehicles were found serviceable including two water carts, a limber, a cart belonging to the Rocket Battery, and three of the 'Scotch' carts customarily used for carrying ammunition boxes. Durnford's body and those of Robert Bradstreet and Durrant Scott were still recognisable. 'Offy' Shepstone, George's brother, removed some rings and a pocket knife from that of Durnford: Durnford's watch had been recovered from his body on the night of the battle by one of Chelmsford's doctors and sent

to Bishop Colenso. It was later claimed by Durnford's brother, Edward, that 'Offy' Shepstone had also removed papers from Durnford's body. Edward Durnford accepted Shepstone's denial, though Colenso's daughter, Frances, refused to do so and the matter ended in a court of inquiry in 1886 as a result of pressure exerted by another engineer officer, Lieutenant-Colonel C. E. Luard. Shepstone, however, was acquitted of any wrongdoing and Luard was forced to apologise.

In fact, some papers of Durnford were recovered from the battlefield by a Trooper Pearse of the Natal Carbineers, but they consisted primarily of the order directing Durnford to move to Rorke's Drift on 19 January and a hand-written copy of Chelmsford's instructions for column commanders dating from December 1878. Edward Durnford went on to defend his brother's reputation in a pamphlet in 1880 and a book two years later. Godwin-Austen's body was also recognisable while a number of witnesses, including Trooper Miles Gissop of the 17th Lancers, saw 'two little drummer boys locked in each others' arms in death'. A persistent story originating at the time of Chelmsford's return to the camp on the night of 22 January had been that two drummer boys had been hung up on butcher's hooks and disembowelled alive but this seems unlikely. Gissop also remarked on the wagons still with the remains of their oxen or mules yoked as well as the remnants of tents, stores and ammunition boxes scattered about.

War correspondents also accompanied the group to Isandlwana, Archibald Forbes of the *Daily News* recording his impressions of a scene that was still grim despite the passage of time. He observed the artillery horses dead in their traces in the ravine in which the gun had stuck, and the dismembered remains of the defenders lying where they fell, 'like a long string with knots in it, the string formed of single corpses, the knots of clusters of dead ...' It was a sobering sight: 'Some were wholly dismembered, heaps of yellow clammy bones. I forbear to describe the faces, with their blackened features and beards bleached by rain and sun. Every man had been disembowelled. Some were scalped and others subjected to yet ghastlier mutilations. The clothes had lasted better than the poor bodies they covered, and helped to keep the skeletons together.' There was also other debris including 'brushes, toilet bags, pickle bottles, and unbroken tins of preserved meats and milk'. For Melton Prior of *The Illustrated London News*, the scene was far worse than any other battlefield he had witnessed over seven different campaigns: 'Here I saw not the bodies, but the skeletons of men whom I had known in life and health, some of whom I had known well, mixed up with the skeletons of oxen and horses, and with wagons thrown on their side, all in the greatest confusion, showing how furious had been the onslaught of the enemy. Amidst the various articles belonging to them which were scattered over the field of carnage, were letters from wives at home to their husbands, from English fathers and mothers to their sons, portraits of those dear to them, and other homely little things, remembrances of the dearest associations.' Norris-Newman, who inspected the ruins of his old tent, the bodies of his servants and the skeletons of his horses, equally described bodies in 'all conditions of decay'. There were all manner of objects in the grass and the crops, which had now sprouted from mealie bags torn open at the time.

Because of the hardness of the ground and the lack of suitable tools, bodies or, rather, remains were gathered up and covered with stone cairns. The bodies of the 24th were left alone at Glyn's request until the regiment itself could bury its own, a decision that struck many as 'very strange'. Eventually, interment of the 24th took place on 20 June 1879 under the supervision of the newly promoted Lieutenant-Colonel Wilsone Black. Some additional clearing was undertaken in September 1879, at which time the staffs and a case from the missing Queen's and Regimental Colours of the 2/24th were found, but the battlefield was not finally cleared until March 1880. Relics, including bones, however, were revealed regularly by the rains, as Mitford noted in 1882: 'In spite of a luxuriant growth of herbage the circles where stood the rows of tents are plainly discernible, while strewn about are tent pegs, cartridge cases, broken glass, bits of rope, meat tins and sardine boxes pierced with assegai stabs, shrivelled up pieces of shoe-leather, and rubbish of every description; bones of horses and oxen gleam white

Left: The return of the Queen's Colour of the 1/24th after its recovery from the Buffalo River by a party under the command of Major Wilsone Black. (National Army Museum)

and ghastly, and here and there in the grass one stumbles upon a half-buried skeleton.'

Many of the cairns were reconstructed in early 1883, at which time the body of Anstey was removed for reburial by his family: Durnford had been reburied by the Colenso family in Pietermaritzburg in October 1879. Memorials to the colonial units were erected after the war, and one to the 24th unveiled in 1914, was built over one of the larger original cairns. The cairns appear only to have been whitewashed after 1900. It was not until 1928 that the area containing most of the cairns was fenced off, and many outside this area were lost over the years in the sense that they became indistinguishable from heaps of stones. Some were reconstructed and others located and recorded in 1958, though some of these latter cairns marking the likely vicinity of the death of Dyson and his section have also since been lost. Many of the Zulu dead were buried in dongas, antbear holes and the mealie-pits of homesteads in the vicinity.

Conceivably, ordinary Zulu did not necessarily comprehend the implications of what had happened at Isandlwana and Rorke's Drift. Cetshwayo, however, was deeply shocked by the casualties inflicted by the British even in defeat and angered that his commanders had allowed the *impi* to attack before its pre-bat-tle rituals had been properly undertaken, and subsequently to disperse. The Zulu losses cannot be known with any certainty and the British probably exag-

Below:
Rorke's Drift. A print
after H. Dupray.

gerated them, but it is estimated that they must have lost at least 1,000 dead at Isandlwana and at least 600 at Rorke's Drift. Ntshingwayo had had two of his sons killed at Isandlwana and the dead also included the chief of the Biyela, Mkhosana kaMvundlana, and Mpande's former chief counsellor, Sigodi kaMasiphula. Many more Zulu were terribly wounded and, though some Zulu were still to be found by travellers like Mitford in 1882, having survived such wounds, it is clear that many did not. Mitford, indeed, commented on how few wounded survivors were to be seen.

On the same day as Isandlwana, Pearson's No 1 Column inflicted a defeat on another Zulu force of between 4,000 and 5,000 men at Nyezane, resulting in perhaps another 300 dead, although Pearson then fortified a position at Eshowe and was effectively besieged there until early April 1879. In the north, Wood's No 4 Column carried out a series of raids from its base at Khambula. While Wood was worsted on one such raid at Hlobane on 28 March, when encountering the main Zulu army of some 20,000 men which Cetshwayo had re-assembled, the subsequent Zulu assault on Wood's entrenchment on the following day resulted in perhaps another 2,000 Zulu dead. Together with the repulse of some 10,000 Zulu sent against Chelmsford's Eshowe relief force at Gingindlovu on 2 April, which cost another 1,000 or so Zulu dead, Khambula ended any hopes Cetshwayo may have entertained of forcing the British to negotiate. Defections increased, notably that of Hamu, referred to earlier. Cetshwayo, therefore, attempted to negotiate in March 1879, but his approaches through Bishop Shreuder were rebuffed by Chelmsford who was anxious for a decisive victory.

Accordingly, with considerable reinforcements having arrived from England, Chelmsford embarked on a second invasion of Zululand on 31 May, spurred on by the knowledge that Wolseley, who was en route to take command, had superseded him. The news of Isandlwana had reached London on 11 February. Chelmsford had called for immediate reinforcements of at least three battalions, two cavalry regiments and a company of engineers, later asking for six battalions. Before receiving this second request, the Cabinet resolved to send out six infantry battalions, two cavalry regiments, two artillery batteries and a company of engineers. It was also decided to send out three senior officers, Major-Generals Henry Crealock, Edward Newdigate and Frederick Marshall, a fourth – Clifford – being added on 27 February. The 6,000 miles separating South Africa from England, of course, meant that it took 60 days for the reinforcements to be landed at the Cape. Durban was another 730 miles from the Cape.

The manner of Chelmsford's removal aroused controversy in some quarters. Clearly still in a state of shock, he himself had requested a designated second in command in letters to the Duke of Cambridge, on 5 and 10 February. Lady Frere, acting under instructions from her husband, who was in Pietermaritzburg, also wrote to the Duke from the Cape on 4 February urg-

ing the appointment of a second in command. Frere had in mind Alison of the War Office Intelligence Branch. Hassard, of course, was incapable of replacing Chelmsford. The highly capable Evelyn Wood was commanding No 4 Column, of course, but he was low on the Colonel's list and, in the view of Cambridge, already over-rewarded for his services in the Ninth Frontier War. There was some confusion for a time as to whether Clifford or Henry Crealock was supposed to be the designated second in command. Clifford was the senior of the two, but was intended to take command of the lines of communication and to sort out the continuing problems of transport. The rather clumsy solution adopted by Cambridge but not really conveyed adequately to either man was that Crealock would act as second in command to Chelmsford in the field, but that Clifford would actually succeed to the command if anything happened to Chelmsford.

In the event, Clifford developed a growing antipathy for Chelmsford, to the extent that there was a dispute in June over Clifford's alteration of one of Chelmsford's telegrams requesting yet more reinforcements. Chelmsford's simmering dispute with Bulwer also continued to escalate. The Cabinet's decision to replace Chelmsford with Wolseley on 26 May solved the problem but only in the longer-term since Wolseley did not reach the Cape until 23 June. Wolseley was to come out with local rank of full general and concurrent appointments as Governor of Natal and the Transvaal and High Commissioner for South-East Africa.

The Duke's exasperation with Chelmsford increased because of the laborious pace of the second advance. Moreover, another disaster had already befallen a convoy escorted by a detachment of the 80th Foot at Ntombe on 12 March. On 1 June Louis Napoleon, the Prince Imperial of France, serving in a voluntary capacity, was killed while out on a small patrol, which added to Chelmsford's woes. The scapegoat this time was Captain J. B. Carey, who had abandoned the Prince to his fate, but Clifford for one felt that Chelmsford also had some responsibility and was evading it. Clifford's criticism became so marked that Cambridge was compelled to reprimand him. Chelmsford, determined to try to regain his reputation before Wolseley could reach the front, pointedly ignored Wolseley's orders that he halt his advance. On 4 July, Chelmsford's force of some 5,500 men advancing in square formation finally shattered some 20,000 Zulu outside Ulundi. Again, it is difficult to gauge precise Zulu losses but possibly more than 1,500 died. It has been claimed that Ulundi was magnified as a victory. It was alleged that the Zulu attack was at best half-hearted and hostilities rapidly ended due to the sheer exhaustion of the Zulu as well as the comparative leniency of the British terms, which made submission acceptable. In fact, the intensity of the Zulu attack was considerable, some reaching within 30 yards of the square despite the overwhelming fire put down by the British. Moreover, the scale of the final defeat was sufficient to prove fatal to Cetshwayo's authority. The Zulu openly acknowledged

Opposite page:
Rorke's Drift – a print
after W. B. Wollen.

defeat and Wolseley received the submissions of the chiefs following Cetshwayo's flight. The Zulu King was eventually run to ground on 28 August 1879. Chelmsford never again commanded in the field, and died of a heart attack while playing billiards in 1905.

The settlement imposed by Wolseley entailed the fragmentation of the kingdom into thirteen separate segments under chiefs regarded as reliable such as Hamu and John Dunn, though Ntshingwayo and Zibhebhu were also among them. By recognising the chiefs and leaving the economic structure unchanged, the British succeeded in making the Zulu monarchy irrelevant to most ordinary Zulu. Cetshwayo, who had visited England in 1882, was allowed to return to Zululand but was forced to flee by attacks from the chiefs established by Wolseley, dying at Eshowe in February 1884 while under the protection of the British Resident. Subsequently the ambitions of individual chiefs were to lead to a civil war, partition and annexation in 1887. Annexation was largely a consequence of the threat of intervention by the Boers of the Transvaal, which had regained its independence as a result of the Anglo-Transvaal or First Boer War of 1880–81. That war itself, of course, was continuing evidence of Frere's mistaken view that the end of Zulu military power would reconcile the Boers to confederation, the contest between Great Britain and the Boers subsequently shaping the evolution of South Africa into the twentieth century.

Amid the wider conflict between the British and the Boers and then the greater conflicts of the twentieth century, the Zulu War was largely forgotten. All that changed, however, with

Zulu, and it has now become the best known of all Britain's colonial campaigns. Isandlwana itself continues to exert its particular fascination, the site being one of the most visited in South Africa. Part of the battlefield of Isandlwana was declared a national monument in 1972 and a larger part finally became a protected historic reserve in 1989. A memorial to the Zulu dead was finally erected

Left: King Cetshwayo surrendering to Major Marter of the 1st King's Dragoon Guards on 28 August 1879. Cetshwayo was exiled to Cape Town. He visited England in 1882 and returned to Zululand in 1884 but died soon afterwards. A contemporary print.

in 1999, taking the form of an *iziqu* or bead 'bravery necklace', close to where many of the Zulu dead were originally buried. That was entirely appropriate, for Isandlwana was much more a Zulu victory than simply a British defeat.

Right: 'Waiting' – a sentry at a fortified camp. Note the Gatling machine-gun at left. An engraving by 'W. I. M.' after W. H. Overend.

APPENDIX I
THE COURT OF INQUIRY

Adjutant-General, camp, Helpmekaar, Natal
January 29, 1879.

Herewith proceedings of court of inquiry, assembled by order of the Lieutenant-General Commanding. The court has examined and recorded the statements of the chief witnesses.

The copy of the proceedings forwarded was made by a confidential clerk of the Royal Engineers.

The court has refrained from giving an opinion, as instructions on this point were not given it.

[Signed] F. C. Hassard, CB,
Colonel Royal Engineers, President.

Proceedings of a Court of Inquiry, assembled at Helpmekaar, Natal, on the 27th January 1879, by order of His Excellency the Lieutenant-General Commanding the Troops in South Africa, dated 24th January 1879.

President – Colonel F. C. Hassard, CB, Royal Engineers.
Members – Lieutenant-Colonel Law, Royal Artillery.
               Lieutenant-Colonel Harness, Royal Artillery.

The court, having assembled pursuant to order, proceeded to take the following evidence:

1st Witness – Major Clery states: I am senior staff officer to the 3rd column, commanded by Colonel Glyn, CB, operating against the Zulus. The General Commanding accompanied this column from the time it crossed the border into Zululand.

On the 20th January 1879 at the camp, Isandula, Zululand, the Lieutenant-General Commanding gave orders to Commandant Lonsdale and Major Dartnell to go out the following morning in a certain direction from camp with their men, i.e., the Native Contingent, and the police and volunteers, part of the 3rd column. On the evening of the following day (the 21st) a message arrived from Major Dartnell that the enemy was in considerable force in his neighbourhood, and that he and Commandant Lonsdale would bivouac out that night. About 1.30 a.m., on the 22nd, a messenger brought me a note from Major Dartnell to say that the enemy was in greater numbers than when he last reported, and that he did not think it prudent to attack them unless reinforced by two or three companies of the 24th Regiment. I took this note to Colonel Glyn, CB, at once; he ordered me to take it on to the General. The General ordered the 2nd Battalion 24th Regiment, the Mounted Infantry, and four guns, to be under arms at once to march. This force marched out from camp as soon as there was light enough to see the road. The Natal Pioneers accompanied this column to clear the road. The General first ordered me to write to Colonel Durnford at Rorke's Drift, to bring his force to strengthen the camp, but almost immediately afterwards he told Colonel Crealock that he (Colonel Crealock) was to write to Colonel Durnford these instructions, and not I. Before leaving the camp I sent written instructions to Colonel Pulleine, 24th Regiment, to the following effect: 'You will be in command of the camp during the absence of Colonel Glyn; draw in [I speak from memory] your camp, or your line of defence' – [I am not certain which] – 'while the force is out; also draw in the line of your infantry outposts accordingly, but keep your cavalry vedettes still far advanced.' I told him to have a wagon ready loaded with ammunition ready to follow the force going out at a moment's notice, if required. I went to Colonel Pulleine's tent just before leaving camp to ascertain that he had got these instructions, and I again repeated them verbally to him. To the best of my memory, I mentioned in the written instructions to Colonel Pulleine that Colonel Durnford had been written to, to bring up his force to strengthen the camp. I saw the column out of camp and accompanied it.

2nd Evidence. – Colonel Glyn, CB, states: From the time the column under my command crossed the border I was in the habit of receiving instructions from the Lieutenant-General Commanding as to the movements of the column, and I accompanied him on most of the patrols and reconnaissances carried out by him. I corroborate Major Clery's statement.

3rd Evidence. – Captain Alan Gardner, 14th Hussars, states: I accompanied the main body of the 3rd column as acting staff officer to officer commanding 3rd column when it left the camp at Isandula on the 22nd January 1879. I was sent back with an order from the General between 10 and 11 a.m. that day into camp, which order was addressed to Colonel Pulleine, and was that the camp of the force out was to be struck and sent out immediately, also rations and forage for about seven days. On arriving in camp I met Captain George Shepstone, who was also seeking Colonel Pulleine, having a message from Colonel Durnford that his men were falling back, and asking for reinforcements. We both went to Colonel Pulleine, to whom I delivered the order. Colonel Pulleine at first hesitated about carrying out the order, and eventually decided that the enemy being already on the hill on our left in large numbers, it was impossible to do so.

The men of the 24th Regiment were all fallen in, and the artillery also, and Colonel Pulleine sent two companies to support Colonel Durnford to the hill on the left, and formed up the remaining companies in line, the guns in action on the extreme left flank of the camp, facing the hill on our left. I remained with Colonel Pulleine by his order. Shortly after, I took the mounted men, by Colonel

Pulleine's direction, about a quarter of a mile to the front of the camp, and left them there under the direction of Captain Bradstreet, with orders to hold the spruit. I went back to Colonel Pulleine, but soon after, observing the mounted men retiring, I went back to them, and, in reply to my question as to why they were retiring, was told they were ordered by Colonel Durnford to retire, as the position taken up was too extended. This same remark was made to me by Colonel Durnford himself immediately afterwards.

By this time the Zulus had surrounded the camp, the whole force engaged in hand-to-hand combat, the guns mobbed by Zulus, and there became a general massacre. From the time of the first infantry force leaving the camp to the end of the fight about one hour elapsed. I estimated the number of the enemy at about 12,000 men. I may mention that a few minutes after my arrival in camp I sent a message directed to the staff officer 3rd column, saying that our left was attacked by about 10,000 of the enemy; a message was also sent by Colonel Pulleine.

The Native Infantry Contingent fled as soon as the fighting began, and caused great confusion in our ranks. I sent messages to Rorke's Drift and Helpmekaar camp that the Zulus had sacked the camp, and telling them to fortify themselves.

4th Evidence. – Captain Essex, 75th Regiment, states: I hand in a written statement of what occurred; I have nothing to add to that statement. [This statement is marked A].

5th Evidence. – Lieutenant Cochrane, 32nd Regiment, states: I am employed as transport officer with No. 2 column, then under Colonel Durnford, RE, on the 22nd January 1879, the column marched on that morning from Rorke's Drift to Isandula in consequence of an order received from the Lieutenant-General. I do not know the particulars of the order received. I entered the Isandula camp with Colonel Durnford about 10 a.m., and remained with him as acting staff officer. On arrival he took over command from Colonel Pulleine, 24th Regiment. Colonel Pulleine gave over to Colonel Durnford a verbal state of the troops in camp at the time, and stated the orders he had received, viz., to defend the camp; these words were repeated two or three times in the conversation. Several messages were delivered, the last one to the effect that the Zulus were retiring in all directions – the bearer of this was not dressed in any uniform. On this message Colonel Durnford sent two troops mounted natives to the top of the hills to the left, and took with him two troops of rocket battery, with escort of one company Native Contingent, on to the front of the camp about four or five miles off. Before leaving, he asked Colonel Pulleine to give him two companies 24th Regiment. Colonel Pulleine said that with the orders he had received he could not do it, but agreed with Colonel Durnford to send him help if he got into difficulties. Colonel Durnford, with two troops, went on ahead and met the enemy some four or five miles off in great force, and, as they showed also on our left, we retired in good order to the drift, about a quarter of a mile in front of the camp, where the mounted men reinforced us, about two miles from the camp. On our retreat we came upon the remains of the rocket battery, which had been destroyed.

6th Evidence. – Lieutenant Smith-Dorrien, 95th Regiment, states: I am transport officer with No. 3 column. On the morning of the 22nd I was sent with a Dispatch from the General to Colonel Durnford at Rorke's Drift; the Dispatch was an order to join the camp at Isandula as soon as possible, as a large Zulu force was near it.

I have no particulars to mention besides.

7th Evidence. – Captain Nourse, Natal Native Contingent, states: I was commanding the escort to the rocket battery when Colonel Durnford advanced in front of the camp, on the 22nd, to meet the enemy. Colonel Durnford had gone on with two troops mounted natives. They went too fast, and left us some two miles in the rear. On hearing heavy firing on our left, and learning that the enemy were in that direction, we changed our direction to the left. Before nearly reaching the crest of the hills on the left of the camp, we were attacked on all sides. One rocket was sent off, and the enemy was on us; the first volley dispersed the mules and the natives, and we retired on to the camp as well as we could. Before we reached the camp it was destroyed.

8th Evidence. – Lieutenant Curling, RA, states: I was left in camp with two guns when the remaining four guns of the battery went out with the main body of the column on 22nd January 1879. Major Stuart Smith joined and took command of the guns about 12 noon.

I hand in a written statement [marked B]. I have nothing to add to that statement.

[Signed] F. C. Hassard,
Colonel, Royal Engineers, President.
F. T. A. Law, Lieutenant-Colonel, RA.
A. Harness, Major, RA and Lieutenant-Colonel.

—

A – Captain Essex's Evidence.

Sir,
I have the honour to forward for the information of the Lieutenant-General Commanding an account of an action which took place near the Isandula Hills on the 22nd instant.

After the departure of the main body of the column nothing unusual occurred in camp until about 8 a.m., when a report arrived from a picket stationed at a point about 1,500 yards distant, on a hill to the north of the camp, that a body of the enemy's troops could be seen approaching from the north-east. Lieutenant-Colonel Pulleine, 1st Battalion 24th Regiment, commanding in camp, thereupon caused the whole of the troops available to assemble near the eastern side of the camp, facing towards the reported direction of the enemy's approach. He also dispatched a mounted man with a report to the column, presumed to be about 12 or 15 miles distant. Shortly after 9 a.m., a small body of the enemy showed itself just over the crest of the hills, in the direction they were expected, but retired a few minutes afterwards, and disappeared. Soon afterwards, information arrived from the picket before alluded to that the enemy was in three columns, two of which were retiring, but were still in view; the third column had disappeared in a north-westerly direction.

At about 10 a.m. a party of about 250 mounted natives, followed by a rocket battery, arrived with Lieutenant-Colonel Durnford, RE, who now assumed command of the camp.

The main body of this mounted force, divided into two portions, and the rocket battery, were, about 10.30 a.m., sent out to ascertain the enemy's movements, and a company of 1st Battalion 24th Regiment, under command of Lieutenant Cavaye, was directed to take up a position as a picket on the hill to the north of the camp at about 1,200 yards distant; the remainder of the troops were ordered to march to their private parades, when the men were to be down in readiness; at this time, about 11 a.m., the impression in camp was that the enemy had no intention of advancing during the daytime, but might possibly be expected to attack during the night. No idea had been formed regarding the probable strength of the enemy's force.

At about 12 o'clock, hearing firing on the hill where the company 1st Battalion 24th Regiment was stationed, I proceeded in that direction. On my way I passed a company of the 1st Battalion 24th Regiment under command of Captain Mostyn, who requested me, being mounted, to direct Lieutenant Cavaye to take special care not to endanger the right of his company, and to inform that officer that he himself was moving up to the left. I also noticed a body of Lieutenant-Colonel Durnford's Mounted Natives retiring down the hill, but did not see the enemy. On arriving at the far side of the crest of the hill, I found the company in charge of Lieutenant Cavaye, a section being detached about 500 yards to the left, in charge of Lieutenant Dyson. The whole were in extended order engaging the enemy, who was moving in similar formation towards our left, keeping at about 800 yards from our line.

Captain Mostyn moved his company into the space between the portions of that already on the hill, and his men then extended and entered into action. This line was then prolonged on our right along the crest of the hill by a body of native infantry. I observed that the enemy made little progress as regards his advance, but appeared to be moving at a rapid pace towards our left. The right extremity of the enemy's line was very thin, but increased in depth towards and beyond our right as far as I could see, a hill interfering with an extended view. About five minutes after the arrival of Captain Mostyn's company, I was informed by Lieutenant Melville [sic], Adjutant 1st Battalion 24th Regiment, that a fresh body of the enemy was appearing in force in our rear, and he requested me to direct the left of the line formed, as above described, to fall slowly back, keeping up the fire. This I did; then proceeded towards the centre of the line. I found, however, that it had already retired. I therefore followed in the same direction, but being mounted, had great difficulty in descending the hill, the ground being very rocky and precipitous. On arriving at the foot of the slope I found the two companies of 1st Battalion 24th Regiment drawn up at about 400 yards distant in extended order, and Captain Younghusband's company in a similar formation in echelon on the left. The enemy was descending the hill, having rushed forward as soon as our men disappeared below the crest, and beyond [?] the right of the line with which I was present had even arrived near the foot of the hill. The enemy's fire had hitherto been very wild and ineffective, now, however, a few casualties began to occur in our line. The companies 1st Battalion 24th Regiment first engaged were now becoming short of ammunition, and at the request of the officer in charge I went to procure a fresh supply, with the assistance of Quartermaster 2nd Battalion 24th Regiment and some men of the Royal Artillery. I had some boxes placed on a mule cart and sent it off to the companies engaged, and sent more by hand, employing any men without arms. I then went back to the line, telling the men that plenty of ammunition was coming. I found that the companies 1st Battalion 24th Regiment before alluded to had retired to within 300 yards of that portion of the camp occupied by the Native Contingent. On my way I noticed a number of native infantry retreating in haste towards the camp, their officers endeavouring to prevent them, but without effect. On looking round to that portion of the field to our right and rear I saw that the enemy was surrounding us. I rode up to Lieutenant-Colonel Durnford, who was near the right, and pointed this out to him. He requested me to take men to that part of the field and endeavour to hold the enemy in check; but while he was speaking, those men of the Native Contingent who had remained in action rushed past us in the utmost disorder, thus laying open the right and rear of the companies of 1st Battalion 24th Regiment on the left, and the enemy dashing forward in the most rapid manner poured in at this part of the line. In a moment all was disorder, and few of the men of 1st Battalion 24th Regiment had time to fix bayonets before the enemy was among them using their assegais with fearful effect. I heard officers calling to their men to be steady; but the retreat became in a few seconds general, and in a direction towards the road to Rorke's Drift. Before, however, we gained the neck [sic] near the Isandula Hill, the enemy had arrived on that portion of the field also, and the large circle he had now formed closed in on us. The only space which appeared open was down a deep gully running to the south of the road, into which we plunged in great confusion. The enemy followed us closely and kept up with us at first on both flanks, then on our right only, firing occasionally, but chiefly making use of the assegais. It was now about 1.30 p.m.;

about this period two guns with which Major Smith and Lieutenant Curling, RA, were returning with great difficulty, owing to the nature of the ground, and I understood were just a few seconds late. Further on the ground passed over on our retreat would at any other time be looked upon as impracticable for horsemen to descend, and many losses occurred, owing to horses falling and the enemy coming up with the riders; about half a mile from the neck the retreat had to be carried on in nearly single file, and in this manner the Buffalo River was gained at a point about five miles below Rorke's Drift. In crossing this river many men and horses were carried away by the stream and lost their lives; after crossing, the fire of the enemy was discontinued; pursuit, however, was still kept up, but with little effect, and apparently with the view of cutting us off from Rorke's Drift. The number of white men who crossed the river at this point was, as far as I could see, about 40. In addition to these, there were a great number of natives on foot and on horseback. White men of about 25 or 30 arrived at Helpmekaar between 5 and 6 p.m., when, with the assistance of other men joined there, a laager was formed with wagons round the stores. I estimate the strength of the enemy to have been about 15,000. Their losses must have been considerable towards the end of the engagement.

I have, etc.

[Signed] E. Essex,

Captain 75th Regiment,

Sub-Director of Transports.

—

B – From Lieutenant Curling to Officer Commanding No 8.

Sir, Helpmekaar, January 26, 1879

I have the honour to forward the following report of the circumstances attending the loss of two guns of N Brigade, 5th Battery Royal Artillery, at the action of Isandula on January 22. About 7.30 a.m. on that date a large body of Zulus being seen on the hills to the left front of the camp, we were ordered to turn out at once, and were formed up in front of the 2nd Battalion 24th Regiment camp, where we remained until 11 o'clock, when we returned to camp with orders to remain harnessed up and ready to turn out at a minute's notice. The Zulus did not come within range and we did not come into action. The infantry also remained in column of companies. Colonel Durnford arrived about 10 a.m. with Basutos and the rocket battery; he left about 11 o'clock with these troops in the direction of the hills where we had seen the enemy. About 12 o'clock we were turned out, as heavy firing was heard in the direction of Colonel Durnford's force. Major Smith arrived as we were turning out, and took command of the guns; we trotted up to a position about 400 yards beyond the left front of the Natal Contingent camp, and came into action at once on a large body of the enemy about 3,400 yards off. The 1st Battalion 24th Regiment now came up and extended in skirmishing order on both flanks and in line with us.

In about a quarter of an hour Major Smith took away one gun to the right, as the enemy were appearing in large numbers in the direction of the drift, in the stream in front of the camp.

The enemy advanced slowly, without halting; when they were 400 yards off the 1st Battalion 24th Regiment advanced about 30 yards. We remained in the same position. Major Smith returned at this time with his gun, and came into action beside mine. The enemy advancing still, we began firing case, but almost immediately the infantry were ordered to retire. Before we could get away the enemy were by the guns, and I saw one gunner stabbed as he was mounting on to an axle-tree box. The limber gunners did not mount, but ran after the guns. We went straight through the camp but found the enemy in possession. The gunners were all stabbed going through the camp, with the exception of one or two. One of the two sergeants was also killed at this time. When we got on to the road to Rorke's Drift it was completely blocked up by Zulus. I was with Major Smith at this time, he told me he had been wounded in the arm. We saw Lieutenant Coghill, the ADC, and asked him if we could not rally some men and make a stand, he said he did not think it could be done. We crossed the road with the crowd, principally consisting of natives, men left in camp, and civilians, and went down a steep ravine heading towards the river.

The Zulus were in the middle of the crowd, stabbing the men as they ran. When we had gone about 400 yards we came to a deep cut in which the guns stuck. There was, as far as I could see, only one gunner with them at this time, but they were covered with men of different corps clinging to them. The Zulus were on them almost at once, and the drivers pulled off their horses. I then left the guns. Shortly after this I again saw Lieutenant Coghill, who told me Colonel Pulleine had been killed.

Near the river I saw Lieutenant Melville [sic], 1st Battalion 24th Regiment, with a colour, the staff being broken.

I also saw Lieutenant Smith-Dorrien assisting a wounded man. During the action cease fire was sounded twice.

I am, etc.
[Signed] H. T. Curling,
Lieutenant, RA

APPENDIX II
SUPPLEMENTARY STATEMENTS OF EVIDENCE

STATEMENT OF LIEUTENANT-COLONEL J. NORTH CREALOCK,
Acting Military Secretary.

[No date but forwarded by Chelmsford to the Secretary of State for War on 9 February 1879]

1. Soon after 2 a.m. on the 22nd January I received instructions from the Lieutenant-General to send a written order to Lieutenant-Colonel Durnford, RE, commanding No 2 column, to the following effect (I copied it in my notebook, which was afterwards lost): – 'Move up to Isandula Camp at once with all your mounted men and Rocket Battery; take command of it. I am accompanying Colonel Glyn, who is moving off at once to attack Matyana and a Zulu force said to be 12 or 14 miles off, and at present watched by Natal Police, Volunteers, and Natal Native Contingent. Colonel Glyn takes with him 2/24th Regiment, four guns RA, and Mounted Infantry.'

2. I was not present during the conversation between Major Clery, Staff Officer to Colonel Glyn, and the Lieutenant-General, but the evening before, about 8.30 p.m., on this officer asking the Lieutenant-General if the 1/24th 'were to reinforce Major Dartnell in the Magane Valley,' he said 'No.' The General received, I believe through Colonel Glyn, a subsequent representation which caused the fresh orders at 2 a.m. the 22nd, and the orders to Lieutenant-Colonel Durnford.

3. Lieutenant-Colonel Durnford, R. E., was not under Colonel Glyn's command at this time; he had been moved from his original position before Middle Drift with some 250 Mounted Natives, 200 of Sikalis footmen, the Rocket Battery, and one battalion of the 1st Regiment Natal Native Contingent to the Umsinga district, on the Lieutenant-General's seeing the ease with which the Natal frontier could be passed in that part of the Buffalo River. The Lieutenant-General's order was therefore sent to him by me, being the only head-quarter staff officer (except the aide-de-camp) with him. These details formed part of No. 2 column under his command.

4. I sent the orders to him by Lieutenant Smith-Dorrien, of 95th Foot, with directions to leave as soon as he could see his way. I expected him to find Colonel Durnford at the Bashee Valley; it was delivered and acted upon.

5. Although I was not aware at that time of the Lieutenant-General's grounds for ordering the troops from camp, yet it was evident to me that he wished to close up to the camp all outlying troops, and thus strengthen it. He would naturally also consider that the presence of an officer of Colonel Durnford's rank and corps would prove of value in the defence of a camp, if it should be attacked.

6. The Lieutenant-General had himself noticed mounted men in one direction (our left front) on the 21st. A patrol of the Mounted Infantry had found another small body of the enemy in our front, and Major Dartnell, we knew, had a strong force before him on our right front. It was evident to me that the Zulu forces were in our neighbourhood, and the General had decided, on the evening of the 21st, to make a reconnaissance to our left front.

7. It did not occur to me that the troops left in camp were insufficient for its defence. Six companies British Infantry, 2 guns, 4 companies Natal Contingent, 250 Mounted Natives, 200 Siaklis men, and details of Mounted Corps appeared to me – had I been asked – a proper force for the defence of the camp and its stores.

8. I subsequently heard Major Clery state that he had left precise instructions to Lieutenant-Colonel Pulleine 'to defend the camp'. Such instructions would, I consider as a matter of course, be binding on Colonel Durnford on his assuming command of the camp.

9. The first intimation that reached me on the 22nd of there being a force of Zulus in the neighbourhood of the camp was between 9.30 and 10 a.m. We were then off-saddled on a neck [sic] facing the Isipise range, distant some 12 miles from camp. During the three previous hours we had been advancing with Colonel Glyn's column against a Zulu force that fell back from hill to hill as we advanced, giving up without a shot most commanding positions. Major Clery at this time received a half-sheet of foolscap with a message from Lieutenant-Colonel Pulleine informing him (I think it ran) that a Zulu force had appeared on the hills on his left front. Our own attention was chiefly bent on the enemy's force retiring from the hills in our front, and a party being pursued by Lieutenant-Colonel Russell three miles off. This letter was not addressed to me, and I did not note on it the time of receipt, but one I received from Colonel Russell soon after is noted by me (I think, for it is at Pietermaritzburg) as received at 1020.

10. Lieutenant Milne, RN, ADC, shortly after this descended a hill on our left, whence he had been on the look-out with a telescope. All the news he gave regarding the camp was that the cattle had been driven into camp. I believe this to have been nearly 11 a.m.

11. In the meantime information reached the General that the right of our force was smartly engaged with the enemy's left. Two companies of 2/24th and the 2nd battalion of the Natal Native Contingent climbed the hill to our right, and, striking across the flat hill, joined the Volunteers who were still engaged. Colonel Glyn accompanied them, having first ordered back the four guns and two companies 2/24th to the wagon track, with instructions to join him near the Mangane Valley. He had also sent back instructions by Captain Alan Gardner, 14th Hussars, to Lieutenant-Colonel Pulleine. I was not informed of their nature. I took the opportunity of ordering our own small camp to proceed to join us, as the General intended to move camp up to the Mangane Valley, as soon as arrangements could be made.

12. The 1st battalion Natal Native Contingent had been ordered back to camp, and to skirmish through the ravines in case any Zulus were hanging about near the camp.

13. Not a sign of the enemy was now seen near us, and followed by the remaining two companies 2/24th, we climbed the hill and followed the track taken by the others. Not a suspicion had crossed my mind that the camp was in any danger, neither did anything occur to make me think of such a thing until about 1.15, when Hon. Mr. Drummond said he fancied he had heard (and the natives were certain of it) two cannon shots. We were then moving back to choose a camp for the night, about 12 miles distant from Isandula. About 1.45 p.m., however, a native appeared on a hill above us, gesticulating and calling. He reported that heavy firing had been going on round the camp. We galloped up to a high spot, whence we could see the camp, perhaps 10 or 11 miles distant. None of us could detect anything amiss; all looked quiet. This must have been 2 p.m.

14. The General, however, probably thought it would be well to ascertain what had happened himself, but not thinking anything was wrong, ordered Colonel Glyn to bivouac for the night where we stood; and taking with him some 40 Mounted Volunteers proceeded to ride into camp.

15. Lieutenant-Colonel Cecil Russell, 12th Lancers, now joined us, and informed me that an officer of the Natal Native Contingent had come up to him (about 12 noon, I think) when he was off-saddled, and asked where the General was, as he had instructions to tell him that heavy firing had been going on close to the camp. Our whereabouts was not exactly known, but the 2/24th companies were still in sight, and Colonel Russell pointed them out, and said we were probably not far from them. This officer, however, did not come to us.

16. This information from Colonel Russell was immediately followed by a message from Commandant Browne, commanding the 1st battalion Natal Native Contingent, which had been ordered back to camp at 9.30 a.m. – (the battalion was halted a mile from us, and probably eight miles from camp) – to the effect that large bodies of Zulus were between him and the camp, and that his men could not advance without support. The General ordered an immediate advance of the battalion, the Mounted Volunteers and Mounted Infantry supporting it.

17. I am not aware what messages had been sent from the camp and received by Colonel Glyn or his staff; but I know that neither the General nor myself had up to this time received any information but that I have mentioned.

18. At 3.15 the Lieutenant-General appeared to think that he would be able to brush through any parties of Zulus that might be in his road to the camp without any force further than that referred to, viz., 1st battalion Native Contingent and some 80 mounted white men.

19. At 4 p.m., however, the Native battalion again halted and I galloped on to order the advance to be resumed when I met Commandant Lonsdale, who remarked to me as I accosted him, 'The Zulus have the camp.' 'How do you know?' I asked, incredulously. 'Because I have been into it,' was his answer.

20. The truth was now known, and every one drew his own conclusions; mine were unluckily true, that hardly a man could have escaped. With such an enemy and with only foot soldiers it appeared to me very improbable that our force could have given up the camp until they were surrounded.

21. The General at once sent back Major Gossett, ADC, 54th Regiment, to order Colonel Glyn to advance at once with everyone with him. He must have been five or six miles off. It was now 4 p.m. We advanced another two miles, perhaps. The 1st battalion 2nd regiment Natal Native Contingent deployed in three ranks, the first being formed of the white men and those natives who had firearms, the Mounted Volunteers and Mounted Infantry on the flanks, with scouts to the front.

22. About quarter to 5 we halted at a distance, I should think, of two miles from camp, but two ridges lay between us and the camp, and with our glasses we could only observe those returning the way they had come. Colonel Russell went to the front to reconnoitre, and returned about 5.45 with a report that 'All was as bad as it could be'; that the Zulus were holding the camp. He estimated the number at 7,000.

23. The troops with Colonel Glyn had pushed on with all possible speed, though the time seemed long to us as we lay and watched the sun sinking. At 6 p.m. they arrived, and, having been formed into fighting order, were addressed by the General. We then advanced to strike the camp and attack any one we found in our path back to Rorke's Drift.

24. I consider it but just to the Natal Native Contingent to state that it was my belief that evening, and is still the same, that the two battalions would have gone through any enemy we met, even as our own British troops were prepared to do. I noticed no signs of wavering on their part up to sunset, when I ceased to be able to observe them.

[Signed] J. N. Crealock, Lieut-Col.,
Assistant Military Secretary.

—

Statement by Captain Alan Gardner, 14th Hussars

Camp, Rorke's Drift, January 26, 1879.

I left the force with the General about 10.30 a.m. and rode back to Isandula Camp, with the order to Lieutenant-Colonel Pulleine to send on the camp equipment and supplies of the troops camping out, and to remain himself at his present camp, and entrench it. Between 12 and 1 o'clock I reached Isandula, and met captain G. Shepstone, who told me he had been sent by Colonel Durnford for reinforcements; that his (Colonel D's) troops were heavily engaged to the left of the our camp, beyond the hill, and were being driven back. We proceeded together to Colonel Pulleine. I delivered him my order, but the enemy were now in sight at the top of the hill, on our left. Lieutenant-Colonel Pulleine sent out two companies about half-way up the hill, and drew up the remainder, with the two guns in action, in line, on the extreme left of our camp, and facing towards the left, from which direction the enemy were advancing in great numbers. For a short time, perhaps 15 minutes, the Zulus were checked, but soon commenced to throw forward their left, extending across the plain on our front. We had between 30 and 40 mounted men, and I asked permission to take them down in the plain, and check the enemy's turning movement. Lieutenant-Colonel Pulleine told me to do so, and I accordingly galloped them to the front, and lined the spruit running across the front of our camp. The Basutos, who were previously retiring, formed line with us, and the enemy halted and commenced firing from behind cover. Leaving the mounted men, who were under Captain Bradstreet, I returned to Lieutenant-Colonel Pulleine, who had previously told me to remain with him. Shortly afterwards, observing the mounted men retiring, I rode back to ascertain the cause. Captain Bradstreet told me he had been ordered to do so by Colonel Durnford, who soon afterwards told me himself that he considered our position too extended, and wished to collect all the troops together. But it was now too late. Large masses of the enemy were already in the camp, and completely surrounded the men of the 24th Regiment. Numbers of these were also on the road to Rorke's Drift. The guns were limbered up and attempted to retire to the left of that road, but were surrounded and overturned. The few mounted men remaining retreated up the small hill on the right rear of the camp, but were soon surrounded by the enemy advancing from the left and front. Many were killed. A few of us managed to escape by riding down the hill on the right, but many were shot riding along the narrow valley, and more drowned and shot in crossing the Buffalo. When I saw all was lost, I sent an order by a Basuto to the officer on Rorke's Drift, telling him to fortify and hold the house. I also sent a similar order to Helpmekaar. We reached Helpmekaar about 5 p.m., and near a laager round the Commissariat stores I endeavoured to obtain a messenger to go to Colonel E. Wood, as I feared the General's force would be cut off, and hoped he, Colonel Wood, might be in time to lend his assistance. No one would go, the Basutos saying they did not know the way. So on the return of the two companies who had started for Rorke's Drift, I decided on going myself, and riding all night reached Utrecht about 4 o'clock the next day. I then got a messenger to go to Colonel Wood, and returned myself to Helpmekaar. On the road, learning that Colonel Glyn's head-quarters were at Rorke's Drift, I proceeded thither. I trust I may not be thought presumptuous if I state my opinion, that had there been a regiment or even two squadrons of cavalry the disaster at Isandula would not have occurred. The enemy's advance across our front, which was requisite in order to turn our right, was in extremely loose order, the ground was an open plain, and could easily have been cleared by a determined charge. The enemy's shooting was so indifferent that our loss would have been very small. The result, moreover, of a cavalry charge would have had a very different effect on the enemy's morale to the retreating fire of mounted skirmishers, and I feel confident we could have held our own till the return of the General's force.

[Signed] Alan Gardner,
Captain, 14th Hussars, Staff Officer,
3rd Column.

—

STATEMENT BY LIEUTENANT W. F. D. COCHRANE,
32nd Light Infantry, Transport Officer, No. 2 Column, to the Assistant Adjutant-General, Head-Quarters, Pietermaritzburg.

Pietermaritzburg,
February 8th, 1879.

Sir,

In compliance with your request, I have the honour to give the account of the battle of Sandhlwana from my own personal observation, and from the information which I have received from reliable sources.

On the morning of the 20th January, 1879, No. 2 Column, to which I had been appointed Transport Officer, was stationed as follows:-

Nos. 1 and 3 Battalions of the 1st Regiment Native Contingent; and one Mounted Troop under Captain Cherry, 32nd Light Infantry at Kranzkop; No. 2 Battalion of the same Regiment under Major Bengough, 77th Regiment, near Sands Spruit, five troops Mounted Men, Russell's Rocket Battery, and two Companies of the 1st Battalion 1st Regiment Natal Native Contingent at Helpmekaar.

Colonel Durnford was commanding this latter portion in person; Capt. Shepstone and I were with Colonel Durnford. Early on the 20th Colonel Durnford marched to Rorke's Drift, crossing the river by means of the Pont, and establishing himself in a camp about half a mile from the river. Here we remained during the 21st. Capt. George Shepstone rode to Sandhlwana Camp and returned same day.

Lieut. Smith-Dorrien rode also to the camp, and returned with a dispatch on the morning of the 22nd instant.

Colonel Durnford was on the road to the Dutch farms, on the Biggarsberg, for the purpose of commanding the Dutchmen's wagons when the dispatch reached him.

I was with Colonel Durnford, and he remarked to me, 'Just what I thought; we are to proceed at once to Sandhlwana. There is an Impi about eight miles from the camp, which the General moves out to attack at daybreak.'

Colonel Durnford returned to Rorke's Drift Camp at once, and marched for Sandhlwana at about 7.30 or 8 a.m.

My orders were to see all the wagons inspanned, start them off, and hand them over to Conductor McCarthy, and then join Colonel Durnford. I complied with these instructions, and arrived at the Sandhlwana Camp with Colonel Durnford about 10 or 10.30 a.m.

Having made all the necessary arrangements for his Column, Colonel Durnford took over the Command from Colonel Pulleine, 1st Battalion 24th Regiment, who gave him a state of the troops, which were:

2 Guns, Royal Artillery, under Major Smith; 5 Companies, 1st Battalion 24th Regiment; 1st Company, 2nd Battalion 24th Regiment; a few mounted men, and, as I understand, some of Lonsdale's Contingent, numbering about 250 (of these numbers I am not quite certain), and the verbal orders, which were, 'To defend the camp.'

The news was, that a number of Zulus had been seen since an early hour on the top of the adjacent hills, and that an attack had been expected; and in consequence, the following disposition had been made:– The Natives of Lonsdale's Contingent were on outpost duty on the hills to the left; the guns were in position on the left of the camp; the Infantry were turned out, and formed in column in the open space in front of the General's tent.

The wagons, etc., were inspanned. Constant reports came in from the scouts on the hills to the left, but never anything from the men on the top of the Sandhlwana Hill, that I heard. Some of the reports were, 'The enemy are in three columns.' 'The columns are separating, one moving to the left rear, and one towards the General.' 'The enemy are retiring in every direction.'

Upon this latter report, Colonel Durnford said he would go out and prevent the one column joining the Impi, which was supposed at that time to be engaged with the troops under the General. He asked Colonel Pulleine to give him two Companies of the 24th to go with the Natives.

Colonel Pulleine objected, stating that he did not think he would be justified in sending away any men, as his orders were 'To defend the camp.' Colonel Durnford said, 'Very well! perhaps I had better not take them. I will go with my own men.' Previous to this, Colonel Durnford on hearing that one column of the enemy was moving towards the left rear, had reinforced the baggage guard (which at that time consisted of one Company Native Contingent), with one troop of mounted Natives; and I understand that Captain George Shepstone was sent back with this party. Colonel Durnford now sent two troops on the hills to the left, under Captain Barton, Natal Native Contingent, and took with him to the front the remaining two troops, and Russell's Rocket Battery, with a Company of the Natal Native Contingent under Captain Nourse, as escort to the battery. Going at a canter, the Rocket Battery and escort were soon left behind. Having proceeded between 5 and 6 miles, a mounted man came down from the hills on the left, and reported that there was an immense Impi behind the hills to our left, and he had scarcely made the report when the Zulus appeared in force in front of us and to our left; they were in skirmishing order, but 10 or 12 deep, with supports close behind. They opened fire at us at about 800 yards, and advanced very rapidly. We retired some little way, taking up a position in a 'donga' or water-course, of which there are several, across the plain in front of Sandhlwana.

We retired steadily in skirmishing order, keeping up a steady fire for about 2 miles, where we came upon the remains of the Rocket Battery, which had been cut off and broken up; there was a hand-to-hand engagement going on with those that remained. The left wing while retiring was wheeled up to the right and drove the Zulus back, who were not in very large numbers just there at the time. It appears that Captain Russell, whilst following up with the Battery, perceived some of the enemy on his left, he fired three rockets with some effect, this was followed by a volley from the Zulus, the Native Contingent retired, the mules were frightened, and disorder was caused. The enemy seeing this ran down the hill and attacked the Battery. Captain Russell was killed. As the mounted men retired towards them, the Zulus ran back to their cover. The retreat was continued until we arrived at a 'donga', about half a mile in front of the camp. Here a few mounted men, Carbineers, Natal Mounted Police, etc., reinforced our right. A stand was made here, but we were eventually driven in, and the camp was taken from the left. It appears that the mounted men on the left became engaged on the hills about the same time as we were engaged on the flat, and I was informed that they held the Zulus back; but my opinion is that the right of the enemy were only engaging the troops, and did not intend to advance until their left had worked round; and I believe also that Captain Shepstone (who, after the arrival of the baggage, took the troop of mounted natives he had used as escort, on the hills to the left) rode down to the camp, and asked in the name of Colonel Durnford for assistance. This Colonel Pulleine gave him by detaching two Companies of the 24th, a little to the left front.

These, together with the mounted men and Lonsdale's Contingent, fell back into the camp, and, in spite of the artillery fire and the steady musketry of the infantry – who were in good position amongst the stones and boulders to the left, and left centre of the Camp, and who stood their ground most gallantly – the enemy steadily advanced. A general move was made towards the mountain, to take up a last position, but it was too late, the Zulus were too quick and fleet of foot, they caught up the men on foot before they could reach the new position, completely overpowering them by numbers, and assegaing right and left.

The guns moved from left to right across the camp, and endeavoured to take the road to Rorke's Drift; but finding this in the hands of the enemy turned off to the left, came to grief in a 'donga', and had to be abandoned. There was not time to spike them. Major Smith was wounded, but managed to get down to the Buffalo, where, I understand, he was shot.

A few mounted men and a good many natives managed to escape from the camp, but had to ride hard over very rough country to the Buffalo River, a distance of about five miles, under fire from the enemy the whole way. The ground was so bad for horses that the Zulus on foot were able to run as fast as the horses could travel. I should judge that more than half the number that left the camp were killed before they arrived at the Buffalo, and many were drowned, there being no drift, the water running rapidly, with large boulders and deep water alternating.

The officers who escaped consulted together on the road, and decided to form a laager at Helpmekaar.

The fighting lasted from about 11.30 a.m. till 1 p.m., as near as I can judge.

There must have been at least 15,000 Zulus, besides the Reserves, and I should compute the numbers killed at from 2,000 to 2,500. The Zulu system of attack, as represented in the Zulu pamphlet, is easily traceable. The main body being opposite the left centre of the camp; the horns thrown out to the left rear and right front. Had the Zulus completed their scheme, by sending a column to the Buffalo River to cut off the retreat, not a man would have escaped to tell the tale.

As far as I am personally concerned, when I got back to the camp with the mounted men who had been driven out of the 'donga', I found that the enemy had rushed the camp from the left, and were engaged hand-to-hand with the Infantry, who were completely overpowered with overwhelming numbers. I saw that all was over. I made in the direction which I had seen taken by the mounted men, guns Royal Artillery, and the Natives on foot. I was cut off by the enemy, who had now reached the line of retreat; but with a good horse, hard riding, and good luck, I managed to reach the Buffalo River. The Zulus seemed perfectly fearless; they followed alongside, having desperate hand-to-hand fighting with those retreating, mostly our Natives on foot. Many of the enemy were killed between the camp and the river. On several occasions they were quite close to me, but I was fortunate enough to escape whilst others dropped at my side. They fired at us the whole way from the camp to the river, but having mounted the bank on the opposite side we were safe.

I made for Helpmekaar by order of Captains Essex and Gardner, and assisted in forming a laager.

I have, etc.,
[Signed] W. F. D. Cochrane,
Lieut. 32nd Light Infantry,
Transport Officer, No. 2 Column.

SELECT BIBLIOGRAPHY

Printed Primary Sources

Butterfield, P. H. (ed.). *War and Peace in South Africa, 1879–81: the Writings of Philip Anstruther and Edward Essex*. Melville: Strydom, 1987

Child, Daphne (ed.). *The Zulu War Journal of Colonel Henry Harford*. Pietermaritzburg: Shuter & Shuter, 1978

Clark, Sonia (ed.). *Invasion of Zululand, 1879*. Johannesburg: Brenthurst Press, 1979

— *Zululand at War, 1879*. Houghton: Brenthurst Press, 1984

Emery, Frank (ed.). *The Red Soldier: Letters from the Zulu War, 1879*. London: Hodder & Stoughton, 1977

Greaves, Adrian and Best, Brian. *The Curling Letters of the Zulu War*. Barnsley: Pen & Sword Books, 2001

Knight, Ian. *'By the Orders of the Great White Queen': Campaigning in Zululand through the Eyes of the British Soldier, 1879*. London: Greenhill Books, 1992

Laband, John (ed.). *Lord Chelmsford's Zululand Campaign, 1878–9*. Stroud: Sutton, for Army Records Society, 1994

Laband, John and Knight, Ian (eds.). *Archives of Zululand: The Anglo-Zulu War 1879* (London: Archival Publications International, 2000) 6 vols

Preston, Adrian (ed.). *The South African Journal of Sir Garnet Wolseley,1879–80*. Cape Town: Balkema, 1973

Memoirs

Ashe, W. and Wyatt-Edgell, E. V. *The Story of the Zulu Campaign*. London: Sampson Low, Marston, Searle & Rivington, 1880

Bengough, Harcourt. *Memories of a Soldier's Life*. London: Edward Arnold, 1913

Coghill, Patrick. *Whom the Gods Love*. Halesowen: Privately printed, 1983

Durnford, Edward. *A Soldier's Life and Work in South Africa, 1872–79*. London: Sampson Low, Marston, Searle & Rivington, 1882

Fripp, C. E. 'Reminiscences of the Zulu War' in *Pall Mall Magazine* 20, 1900, pp. 547–62

Hallam-Parr, Henry. *A Sketch of the Kafir and Zulu Wars*. London: Kegan Paul, 1880

Hamilton-Browne, G. A. *A Lost Legionary in South Africa*. London: T. Werner Laurie, 1912

Mitford, Bertram. *Through the Zulu Country*. London: Kegan Paul, Trench & Co, 1883

Molyneaux, W. C. F. *Campaigning in South Africa and Egypt*. London: Macmillan, 1896

Moodie, D. C. F. *Moodie's Zulu War*. Cape Town: N & S Press, 1988

Norris-Newman, Charles. *In Zululand with the British Throughout the War of 1879*. London: W. H. Allen, 1880

Smith-Dorrien, Horace. *Memories of Forty-Eight Years' Service*. London: John Murray, 1925

Secondary Sources – Books

Clements, W. H. *The Glamour and Tragedy of the Zulu War*. London: Bodley Head, 1936

Cope, Richard. *Ploughshare of War: The Origins of the Anglo-Zulu War of 1879*. Pietermaritzburg: University of Natal Press, 1999

Coupland, R. *Zulu Battle Piece: Isandhlwana*. London: Collins, 1948

Dominy, Andrew and Ballard, Charles (eds.). *The Anglo-Zulu War: New Perspectives*. Pietermaritzburg: University of Natal Press, 1981

Drooglever, R. W. F. *The Road to Isandlwana: Colonel Anthony Durnford in Natal and Zululand*. London: Greenhill Books, 1992

Edgerton, R. B. *Like Lions They Fought*. Bergvlei: Southern, 1988

French, the Hon. Gerald. *Lord Chelmsford and the Zulu War*. London: John Lane at the Bodley Head, 1939

Furneaux, Rupert. *The Zulu War: Isandhlwana and Rorke's Drift*. London: Weidenfeld & Nicolson, 1963

Gon, Philip. *The Road to Isandlwana: The Years of an Imperial Battalion*. Johannesburg: Donker, 1979

Greaves, Adrian. *Isandlwana*. London: Cassell, 2001

— *Rorke's Drift*. London: Cassell, 2002

Guy, Jeff. *The Destruction of the Zulu Kingdom*. London: Longmans, 1979

Hamilton, Carolyn. *Terrific Majesty*. Cambridge MA: Harvard University Press, 1998

Harrington, Peter. *British Artists and War: The Face of Battle in Paintings and Prints, 1700–1914*. London: Greenhill Books, 1993

Holme, Norman. *The Silver Wreath: Being the 24th Regiment at Isandlwana and Rorke's Drift, 1879*. London: Samson Books, 1979

Knight, Ian. *Brave Men's Blood: The Epic of the Zulu War*. London: Greenhill Books, 1990

— *Zulu: Isandlwana and Rorke's Drift, 22–23 January 1879*. London: Windrow & Greene, 1992

Laband, John. *Kingdom in Crisis: The Zulu Response to the British Invasion of 1879*. Manchester: Manchester University Press, 1992

— *The Rise and Fall of the Zulu Nation*. London: Arms and Armour Press, 1997

Laband, John and Thompson, Paul. *The Buffalo Border, 1879*. Durban: University of Natal, 1983

— *Kingdom and Colony at War*. Pietermaritzburg: University of Natal Press, 1990

Laband, John and Knight, Ian. *The War Correspondents: The Anglo-Zulu War*. Stroud: Sutton, 1996

Lock, Ron and Quantrill, Peter. *Zulu Victory: The Epic of Isandlwana and the Cover Up*. London: Greenhill, 2002

Mackinnon, J. P. and Shadbolt, Sydney. *The South African Campaign, 1879*. London: Sampson Low, Marston, Searle & Rivington, 1882

Morris, Donald. *The Washing of the Spears*. London: Cape, 1966

Rothwell, J. S. *Narrative of The Field Operations Connected with the Zulu War of 1879*. London: HMSO, 1881

Thompson, Paul. *The Natal Native Contingent in the Anglo-Zulu War, 1879*. Pietermaritzburg: Privately printed, 1997

Yorke, Edmund. *Rorke's Drift, 1879: Anatomy of an Epic Zulu War Siege*. Stroud: Tempus, 2001

Secondary Sources – Booklets

Chadwick, George. *The Battles of Isandlwana and Rorke's Drift*. Durban: Privately printed, 1981

Emery, Frank. *The 24th Regiment at Isandhlwana*. Royal Regiment of Wales, 1978

Knight, Ian. *Isandlwana 1879: The Great Zulu Victory*. Oxford: Osprey, 2002

Knight, Ian and Castle, Ian. *Battleground South Africa: Isandlwana*. Barnsley: Pen & Sword Books, 2000

Laband, John. *Fight Us in the Open: The Anglo-Zulu War through Zulu Eyes*. Pietermaritzburg: Shuter & Shuter and the KwaZulu Monuments Council, 1985

Laband, John (ed.). *Companion to the Narrative of Field Operations connected with the Zulu War of 1879*. Constantia: N & S Press, 1989

Laband, John and Matthews, Jeff. *Isandlwana*. Pietermaritzburg: Centaur Publications and the KwaZulu Monuments Council, 1992

Laband, John and Thompson, Paul. *Field Guide to the War in Zululand and the Defence of Natal, 1879*. Pietermaritzburg: University of Natal Press, 1979

— *The Illustrated Guide to the Anglo-Zulu War*. Pietermaritzburg: University of Natal Press, 2000

Whybra, Julian. *The Roll Call: Men Killed in Action and Survivors of Isandlwana and Rorke's Drift*. Reading: Roberts Medals Publications, 1990

Royal Engineers Museum. *Red Earth: The Royal Engineers and the Zulu War, 1879*. Gillingham: Royal Engineers Museum, 1996

Secondary Sources - Articles

Bailes, Howard. 'Technology and Imperialism: A Case Study of the Victorian Army in Africa' in *Victorian Studies*, 24, 1, 1980, pp. 83–104

Castle, Ian. 'The Wretched Campaign of J. C. Russell, 12th Lancers: Zululand, 1879' in *Soldiers of the Queen*, 100, 2000, pp. 12–20

Chadwick, George. 'The Anglo-Zulu War of 1879: Isandlwana and Rorke's Drift' in *Military History Journal*, 4, 4, 1978, pp. 1–21

Clammer, David. 'The Recollections of Miles Gissop: With the 17th Lancers in
    Zululand' in *Journal of the Society for Army Historical Research*, 58, 234,
    1980, pp. 78–92

Coghlan, Mark. 'The World's Biggest Battle Picture' in *Soldiers of the Queen*, 84,
    1996, pp. 12–16

Cooper, Barbara. 'George Hamilton-Browne: An Investigation into his Career in
    New Zealand' in *Historical Review: Bay of Plenty Journal of History*, 33, 2,
    1985, pp. 76–82

Drooglever, R. W. F. 'Charles Fripp and "The Battle of Isandhlwana"' in *Soldiers
    of the Queen*, 70, 1992, p. 5

England, Raimond and Gardiner, Andrew. 'Isandlwana, 22 January 1879:
    Further Observations on Colonel Durnford's No 2 Column' in *Soldiers of the
    Queen*, 65, 1991, pp. 24–7

Guy, Jeff. 'A Note on Firearms in the Zulu Kingdom with special reference to
    the Anglo-Zulu War, 1879' in *Journal of African History*, 12, 4, 1971, pp.
    557–70

Jackson, F. W. D. 'Isandhlwana, 1879: The Sources Re-examined' in *Journal of
    the Society for Army Historical Research*, 43, 173/175/176, 1965, pp. 30–43,
    113–32, 169–83

— 'The First Battalion, Twenty-Fourth Regiment marches to Isandlwana' in Ian
    Knight, ed., *There Will Be An Awful Row At Home About This*. Shoreham-by-
    Sea: Zulu Study Group of the Victorian Military Society, 1987, pp. 2–10

Jackson, F. W. D. and Whybra, Julian. 'Isandhlwana and the Durnford Papers'
    in *Soldiers of the Queen*, 60, 1990, pp. 18–32

Jones, Huw. 'The Durnford Papers: Some Questions and Answers' in *Soldiers
    of the Queen*, 62, 1990, pp. 20–3

Knight, Ian, ed, 'The Last of the 24th, Isandlwana' in *Awful Row At Home*, 1987,
    p. 11

— 'The Zulu Army, 1879' in Ian Knight, ed., *Awful Row At Home*, 1987, pp.
    37–44

— 'R. T. Moynan's Painting, "The Last of the 24th Isandlwana"' in *Journal of the
    Society for Army Historical Research*, 66, 267, 1988, pp. 155–6

— 'Kill Me in the Shadows: The Bowden Collection of Anglo-Zulu War Oral
    History' in *Soldiers of the Queen*, 74, 1993, pp. 9–18

— 'Ammunition at Isandlwana: A Reply' in *Journal of the Society for Army
    Historical Research*, 73, 296, 1995, pp. 237–50

— 'Old Steady Shots: The Martini-Henry Rifle, Rates of Fire and Effectiveness in
    the Anglo-Zulu War' in *Journal of the Anglo-Zulu War Historical Society*, 11,
    2002, pp. 1–5

— 'Secrets of the Dead: The Mysteries of Zulu Dawn' in *Journal of the Anglo-
    Zulu War Historical Society*, 11, 2002, pp. 34–7

Laband, John. 'Zulu Strategic and Tactical Options in the face of the British
    Invasion of January 1879' in *Scientia Militaria*, 28, 1, 1998, pp. 1–15

Below:
The distinctive shape of Isandlwana may be seen in the distance in this photograph taken from Rorke's Drift. (National Army Museum)

Thompson, Paul. 'The Natal Native Contingent at Rorke's Drift, January 22, 1879' in Ian Knight, ed., *Awful Row At Home*, 1987, pp. 12–16 (Also in Laband and Thompson, *Kingdom and Colony at War*, pp. 131–43)

Whybra, Julian. 'Contemporary Sources on the Composition of the Main Zulu Impi, January 1879' in *Soldiers of the Queen*, 53, 1988, pp. 13–16

— 'The Ten Gunners' in *Soldiers of the Queen*, 54, 1988, pp. 2–4

— 'The Ten Gunners: Addenda' in *Soldiers of the Queen*, 58/59, 1990, p. 13

— 'No 1 Squadron Imperial Mounted Infantry, May 1877–January 1879' in *Soldiers of the Queen*, 58/59, 1990, pp. 27–36

Yorke, Edmund. 'Isandlwana, 1879: Reflections on the Ammunition Controversy' in *Journal of the Society for Army Historical Research*, 72, 292, 1994, pp. 205–18

INDEX